PRAISE FOR
COACHING GIRLS' BASKETBALL

"Coach Simpson's book does a brilliant job of synthesizing all the different elements of successful coaching in a fun and informative way. While most coaching books concentrate on either teaching fundamentals or on pure philosophy, this book manages to integrate both. Simpson's insights into effective coaching and breakdown of the game are as good as it gets."

—Charli Turner Thorne,
Head Women's Basketball Coach, Arizona
State University

"In addition to the teaching of the game, *Coaching Girls' Basketball* covers a variety of issues affecting female athletes. This book will help coaches at all levels to coach girls more effectively."

—Mary Hile-Nepfel, Head Basketball
Coach, University of San Francisco

"A valuable tool for all beginning coaches. Sandy Simpson has managed to condense more than 30 years of playing and coaching experiences into a clear, concise, and complete basketball handbook."

—Jorja E. Hoehn, three-time NCAA DII
National Coach of the Year, former
women's basketball coach

"*Coaching Girls' Basketball* is what every youth coach needs to excel in the sport and develop positive relationships with players, parents, and fans. Sandy Simpson has meshed the fundamentals of the game with a comprehensive review of what girls deal with in sports, to help you coach them to their fullest potential."

—Caren Horstmeyer,
Head Women's Basketball Coach,
University of California, Berkeley

COACHING GIRLS' BASKETBALL

COACHING GIRLS' BASKETBALL

From the How-To's of the Game to Practical Real-World Advice—Your Definitive Guide to Successfully Coaching Girls

SANDY L. SIMPSON

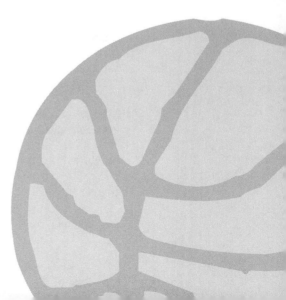

THREE RIVERS PRESS
NEW YORK

Published by Three Rivers Press, New York.
Member of the Crown Publishing Group, a division of Random House, Inc.
www.randomhouse.com

THREE RIVERS PRESS and the Tugboat design are registered trademarks of Random House, Inc.

Originally published by Prima Publishing, Roseville, California, in 2001.

Illustrations: Pamela Tanzey and Andrew Vallas

Printed in the United States of America

Library of Congress Cataloging-in-Publication Data
Simpson, Sandy L.
    Coaching girls' basketball : from the how-to's of the game to practical real-world advice, your definitive guide to successfully coaching girls / Sandy L. Simpson.
        p. cm.
    Includes index.
    1. Basketball for girls—Coaching.   I. Title.

GV886.2 .S56 2001
796.323'8—dc21   2001034041

ISBN 0-7615-3248-X

10 9 8 7 6

First Edition

Dedicated to life's light, my wife Chris, whose love, patience, and unwavering support allow me to pursue a profession I cherish; though not nearly as much as I do her.

CONTENTS

ACKNOWLEDGMENTS

I WISH TO ACKNOWLEDGE the following people who made this book possible in one manner or another.

To Olivia and Sebastian, whose daily antics both amuse and ground me. Much of my sanity comes from them. I love you both!

To my mother, Donna Simpson, who learned about single parenthood before it was prevalent, and did an astonishing job. And, to my baby sister, Pam Ortega, who has managed to defy birth order to become a role model for me. She's as fine a parent as I know.

My three primary mentors in coaching have been Pam Gill-Fisher, Joyce Sake, and Jorja Hoehn. Each gave me a separate gift that embodied who they are and in doing so made me professionally rich beyond warrant.

My three basketball coaches were Bob Hamilton, Bill Wilkin, and Owen Lucey. They taught from the heart and I learned so much from them, but didn't realize how much until years later.

Thank you to all the players I was blessed enough to work with through the years. Almost all did something to make me a better person and to stoke the passion for teaching and coaching this game.

INTRODUCTION

HERE'S THE THING: From all the contests in all the sports that I participated in as a boy, I'm not sure I can extract more than a handful of memories from actual games with any sort of clarity. I can remember the sound of the baseball hitting my mitt and the feel of its seams beneath my fingers as I warmed up to pitch at Beresford Park in San Mateo, California. I can recall being hit so hard by Michael Adams in a tackling drill that any thought of pursuing football as a career vanished prior to hitting the turf. There was the teasing and camaraderie on the bus as our basketball team traveled to nearby high school tournaments. There was the "baseball" free-throw shooting game Dave Perez and I made up to amuse ourselves at practice, and my vain efforts to stop the "floater" shots of basketball teammates Kevin McCoy and Mark Drisko, a dumb little game that, nevertheless, could render us unable to speak as we lay on the floor paralyzed by laughter.

But, most of all, I remember my coaches.

Bill Wilkin, Owen Lucey, and Bob Hamilton. Not household names as determined by our system of American pop culture, but critical figures in helping me mature, establish a value system, and come to appreciate the extraordinary rewards of being part of a group effort. I'm not sure that I appreciated at the time why they dedicated so much of their time to us. Nor could I comprehend what possessed them to care so fervently. I just remember appreciating it. And my gratitude has grown with the passing years.

My own coaching career was not borne of a stellar playing career. Labeling my basketball career "mediocre" would be a gross overstatement. Pursuing coaching as a means to prolong the glory of my association with the game was, therefore, decidedly not a factor. Rather, it was the desire to understand why the coaching models in my life did what they did for me and for other players. Where did their passion come from? Why did they devote incredible amounts of time to our pursuits?

I should say, at this point, that I have never bought into the myth that sport builds character. Rather, I believe, sport reveals character through its clever amalgam of success and disappointment, adversity and prosperity. Through sports, one finds out who the sturdiest among us are. That's not to say that participation in sports cannot help us grow. Modeling is a tremendous agent for change, and, so, in the end it is our associations, the people we play with and learn from, who have the greatest potential for positive influence.

Fortunately, my early coaching career was favored by a few wonderful mentors who helped me understand the role of coach as educator. Pam Gill-Fisher, Joyce Sake, and Jorja Hoehn are as different from each other as are Barbra Streisand, Whitney Houston, and Britney Spears, but each, in her own fashion guided me to the understanding that, to be an effective coach, you need to care more about the person than about the athlete. This tenet holds true at every level of coaching, from youth sports to professional. Watching a young person grow, learn about teamwork, discipline, and establishing goals is an awe-inspiring process. Feeling that you have made a difference in a young person's life is an incredible gift. To this day, the most rewarding aspect of coaching is receiving a genuine hug from a former player.

I am forever grateful to all the positive coaching models in my life, not because they made me a better player or coach, but because they helped me become a better husband and father.

POPULARITY OF GIRLS' BASKETBALL

Girls' basketball is one of the fastest growing segments of the sports scene. According to Youth Basketball of America, nearly 10 million girls, ages 6–17, participated in organized basketball in 1997.

Participation growth at the high school and junior high school levels owes much to Title IX, the landmark 1972 legislative act that made gender equity in our educational system (including school sports) the law. As recently as 1970, according to the Womens' Sports Foundation, only 1 in 27 high school aged girls played varsity sports of any kind. Today that number is 1 in 3.

The recent explosive growth in the number of girls playing youth basketball (ages 6–13) is a response to the need for more, and earlier, opportunities for young girls to play organized basketball in preparation for the secondary school years. Consider it the trickle-down effect of Title IX, and the trend grows stronger with every passing year.

BENEFITS OF SPORTS FOR YOUNG GIRLS

There is no substitute for fun! While an argument (specious though it may be) might be made for emphasizing winning at the higher levels (college and professional) of sport, youth sports (ages 7–13), must be fun if it is to hold any true value. In survey after survey of youth sports participants, two reasons emerged when athletes were asked what they liked best about playing organized sports. First, it's fun. It is truly play for this age group, and the game is just that—a game. Second, these youngsters like making new friends or playing with their current pals. The social aspect of participation is a huge motivator for young children. A third response, somewhat less important to them, was skill development. Kids mentioned that learning more about the sport and how to play well were a source of satisfaction as well. Conspicuous in their absence for most respondents were the concepts of challenge and competition. While inherent in the nature of most games, they rank well down on the list of reasons why children enjoy participation in sports.

Having fun sounds easy enough. What could possibly prevent kids from enjoying themselves on the court or playing field? Not surprisingly, topping the list is pressure. Pressure from parents. Pressure from coaches. Pressure to win. Many children believe that the adults (parents and coaches) involved in youth sports take things too seriously and place too great an emphasis on performance and winning. We have all read recently about what seems to be an increasing spate of violent incidents in youth sports involving parents, coaches, and sometimes umpires and referees. Much of this stems from the overemphasis by parents and coaches on winning at the youth sport level. This is where modeling can have its greatest positive impact. A highly competitive athletic program may be appropriate for a high schooler, but for a nine-year-old girl, the skewed emphasis may do more harm than good.

Coaches (and parents) should adopt a philosophy of support and encouragement. Effort, hustle, and sportsmanship should be rewarded for their own sake. Praise good performance, of course, but refrain from yelling at or belittling poor performance. Constructive feedback and corrective techniques are valued by kids, but only if offered in an atmosphere devoid of judgment. Stay positive!

Of course, if having fun and making friends were all we wanted our kids to get out of an activity, there would be little reason to organize youth sports. Playing sandlot baseball or pick-up basketball would serve the same purpose. Organized sports, however, offer a more structured environment for learning some life skills as well. Among the most important:

- **Self-discipline.** Organized sports offer a structure that requires a commitment to a specific schedule. Practices are slated. Games are scheduled. The self-discipline needed to be places on time and to practice the skills needed to improve instill a sense of responsibility *to* others. Further, young athletes begin the process of learning how to become more disciplined mentally. We may not feel like playing basketball today, but we've made a commitment to the team, and they are depending on us to show up and do our part. We might not like the position the coach has us playing just now, or the coach isn't letting us play at the same time as our friends, but sports help us learn to make the best of a given situation, even at the younger age levels.

- **Sportsmanship.** This primary value of sport can only be imparted through modeling. As a coach, do you teach your players sportsmanship (to do the right thing) or gamesmanship (winning at all costs)? Do you go beyond discussing, by demonstrating, respect for opponents and peers? Do you teach your athletes to respect the game as well? There is a right way and a wrong way to go about things, and the line is clearly marked for all but the most unwitting adults.

- **Cooperation.** While self-discipline and sportsmanship are the provinces of almost any sport, cooperation is best learned in a team sport environment. Your commitment becomes not just to yourself or to a schedule, but to teammates as well. The satisfaction of learning to work well with others is, of course, a critical life skill. It is also one learned faster and more concretely by some than by others. Be patient with kids who have a difficult time grasping this concept at first, because children mature at vastly different rates. It is one of the most important benefits of organized sports.

- **Selflessness.** This goes hand in hand with cooperation and is also best absorbed in a team sport environment. Being able to subjugate at least a portion of our own self-interests is one of the most difficult skills to learn. All of us are self-centered by nature, and 8-, 9-, and 10-year-olds have it refined to an art (later, in adolescence, it will take the form of genius!). Only by constantly reinforcing the value of selflessness will we have any chance of helping it sink in. It is amazing what a group can accomplish when no one cares who gets the credit. De-emphasize the ego-oriented approach that causes children to focus on the rewards that sport offers them. Instead, endeavor to instill the intrinsic rewards of helping a teammate or sacrificing for the sake of the group.

Self-Esteem

We have all witnessed examples of a talented athlete being outplayed by someone who seems to display an outsized will to win. These hard-working, self-possessed athletes are seen at nearly every level, from youth sports to professional, and they all have one thing in common . . . high self-esteem. Does high self-esteem mean feeling as if you can accomplish anything if you put your mind to it? Yes and no. Feeling good about oneself is an obvious benefit when facing a challenge, and sports offer plenty of those. But the true benefit of self-esteem is in the ability to evaluate more astutely one's abilities and limitations and to take responsibility for one's actions rather than making excuses. In short, it is the ability to learn from success and failure in equal measure and to grow from either experience. The constant paradigm of challenge, effort, and outcome presented by sport creates an invaluable environment for developing self-esteem.

For young girls, the tangent issues of self-esteem hold broader, and potentially more serious, ramifications. This is particularly true with regard to body image and the issue of eating disorders, which, while present in males, are far more prevalent in females. We will discuss both of these concepts in greater length in chapter 3.

AUTHOR'S EXPERIENCE

Serendipity is a wonderful concept. Without it, I would never have entered the coaching profession, a service that has provided me with memories and relationships I could not imagine enjoying in any other line of work. More important, it has provided me with a passion accompanied by a living wage. We all fancy waking up each morning excited about going to work. . . . I'm fortunate to live that dream every day.

While I've spent most of my coaching career working at the university level, I had the opportunity some time ago to work with a team of sixth-grade girls for a couple of years. In addition, we run summer youth basketball camps for girls, and I find the contrast between working with college athletes and young girls to be quite invigorating. The chance to be in on the ground floor of some young player experiencing her first successes and beginning to build her confidence is a true joy. It is the ability to make a strong difference that makes working with young athletes so fulfilling.

PHILOSOPHY OF THIS BOOK

Keep in mind that while this book is geared toward the coaching of youth basketball players from ages 7 to 13, no single approach would be applicable to that entire age range. Physical, emotional, and developmental stages vary wildly from age 7 to age 13. In other words, you cannot coach a team of 7-year-olds in the same way you would a group of 13-year-olds.

In general, this book takes the approach that, with the youngest players (ages 7–10), the emphases should be on skill development and making the game fun. The primary goal with younger athletes is to give them a positive experience that will result in them wanting to continue playing the sport. As these players mature and their skills develop, the competitive aspect of the game will become more of a factor. Older players (ages 11–13) are better equipped to handle increasingly complex drills and skills and more sophisticated offensive and defensive systems. Even then, it is important not to let competition and an emphasis on winning become overriding concerns. Make it fun for your players, and they will respond positively to your efforts at every turn.

Designating young athletes into two age groups, one 7–10 years and another 11–13 years, is not an arbitrary act. The physical and psychosocial developmental levels can be worlds apart throughout this age range. Naturally, developmental rates differ from girl to girl; some 10-year-olds are more nature than some 12-year-olds and may be ready for a more competitive environment. As their coach, you are in the best position to determine what your players are ready for competitively. Just remember, in adhering to this book's philosophy, even with the older girls, competition should be well down the list of priorities when developing these young athletes.

I concentrate on the basics in this book. Youth basketball is all about helping players develop a love for the game and learning the basic skills of basketball. If you're looking for tips on sophisticated defensive systems like match-up zones or intricate, multi-optional half-court offensive sets, then this is not the book for you. I will address what it takes to install an offensive or defensive system in Chapter 9, and we will look at various options, but the emphasis, again, will be on simplicity and fundamentals.

HOW TO USE THIS BOOK

Every effort has been made to make this book as user-friendly as possible. Feel free to scan it by chapter topic or by specific subcategory. The first three chapters deal with the aspects of building a program and a coaching philosophy. Included here are sections on roles, communication, coaching traits, discipline, motivation, and many of the issues that deal specifically with coaching young girls. Chapter 4 explains the game's basics in terms of equipment, rules, and the different player positions. Chapters 5–10 focus on broad topics such as conditioning, practice planning, developing fundamental skills, offense, defense, transition, and game coaching.

The figures throughout the book are simple and easy to follow. Figure 4.1 (on page 45) offers a "key" to player and ball movement symbols that will assist you in understanding the figures.

The appendix provides resources that you can use to learn more about coaching basketball.

So read on, enjoy, and never lose sight of the concept that coaching basketball should be fun not only for the girls fortunate enough to have a dedicated mentor, but also for you too. In the end, it's not the destination, but the journey that counts.

COACHING GIRLS' BASKETBALL

1

SO YOU WANT TO BE A COACH?

SO WHAT EXACTLY is a coach? If you think of a coach as an educator and a facilitator, you are well on your way to developing a successful approach to coaching. As a teacher, you will guide, encourage, teach technical skills, help players develop social skills, and set reasonable goals for players to strive toward. As a facilitator, you will attempt to create an environment conducive to learning and to trying new challenges. If your athletes feel secure and comfortable, they will be far more likely to take on risks and to grow from the experience.

While success can be measured in many forms, a coach is often evaluated in terms of his or her wins and losses. That is the nature of the beast, and at the higher levels of sport (high school and beyond) it is reasonable to expect that the coach's winning record will be at least a partial evaluative component. But at the youth sport level, winning should be well down on the list of criteria when determining the relative success of a team or coach. Answer these six questions positively at the end of the season and consider yourself an unmitigated success!

1. Did the players have fun?
2. Did the players' skills improve over the course of the season?

1

3. Did the team performance improve over the course of the season?

4. Did the players' self-esteem improve over the course of the season?

5. Was there a sense of cooperation, selflessness, and sportsmanship on the team?

6. Will the players continue to play the following season?

Don't fool yourself into thinking you will reach every youngster and see dramatic improvement with every player. You probably won't. Some young girls come from complex circumstances that make it difficult to reach them. But you should always try. Just as you ask your athletes to give their best effort, you will always be a success if you give yours.

THE COACH AS LEADER

In accepting the position of head coach, you also accept the mantle of leadership for your team and program. However, leading a team is not as simple as taking a third-grade class on a field trip to the zoo. You cannot have them hold hands as you lead them from challenge to challenge or game to game and expect them to develop into a competitive, cohesive unit as the season progresses. So what exactly is your leadership role as head coach?

Well, first, try to forget about leading and, as mentioned earlier, focus on facilitating. Players lead teams, coaches cultivate leaders. X's and O's aside, your crucial responsibility as coach is to provide structure and to create an atmosphere conducive to team success. It is much like parenting. Can you help each individual player reach her full potential? Can you convince your athletes that subjugating themselves to The Team will provide them with opportunities for fulfillment not available to mere individuals? Can you motivate your players to play with love and passion? What it comes down to is this: Leadership is not directing athletes, it's inspiring them.

Any techno-coach can design a practice, prepare a game plan, and install an offensive or defensive system. While all of those components are important aspects of coaching, if you wish to "lead," here are some things to consider:

Leadership Is Earned, Not Conferred

A coaching title does not ensure leadership status. Real leadership is the ability to inspire and influence players. While leadership from within the team can only emerge over time, as coach, you have an inherent responsibility to provide your team with a framework for success. Credibility comes from observed actions, not words. Honesty and integrity are the keys. Compromise either and you risk losing your players.

Those who possess drive, expertise, and a genuine caring for their players and staff will lead, regardless of their title. Conversely, coaches without the requisite leadership skills may hold positions of authority, but their influence will seldom extend beyond exacting compliance with what is minimally expected. In other words, you want your players to play for themselves and for each other, but you also hope they are playing a little bit for you, too.

Coaching Tip

Don't tell your players who you are, show them. If you are emotive and intense, go with it, but channel all that energy positively. If you are reserved by nature, be a coach of few words. A look speaks volumes. Avoid trying to be someone you're not. Young kids are very intuitive and can spot a phony a half-court shot away.

Be True to Your Philosophy and Core Values

You can view this in terms of both your basketball philosophy and your standards for conduct. Players are smart. They "read" coaches quickly. If you don't believe in your system, there's no reason for the team to buy into what you're doing either. This doesn't mean you can't let your philosophies evolve. It simply means avoiding the confusion that can accompany frequent and abrupt shifts in direction. If you believe, for example, in the defensive system you have installed, don't be too quick to abandon it if success eludes the team early on. That's why you practice. If you know it works, your players will eventually make it work. On the other hand, don't be mulishly stubborn about tweaking your system or even making sweeping changes if the situation obviously warrants it. So, how do you know when to stick to your guns and when to make changes for the good of the team? Ah, well, that is part of the art of coaching. And, as with any artist, sometimes you will fail miserably. Through that failure, you will grow as a coach.

When it comes to your philosophy on standards of behavior, team discipline, rules, and the like, however, consistency is an absolute must. If you have a team rule, be prepared to enforce it, pure and simple. Double standards are cancerous concepts. They reflect poorly on your integrity and will undermine your authority more quickly than anything else you might do. Focus on "values": honesty, effort, sportsmanship, respect, and consideration for others. Hold your players accountable for their actions. Don't sweat the small stuff. Shirt tails, hairstyles, sock length, headbands, and other cosmetic accouterments are trend-based and are constantly evolving. Be flexible and change with the times to the greatest degree you're comfortable with. Can you "draw the line" on some of these forms of expression? Sure. Just try to avoid micro-managing the spirit from your team.

Be Willing to Listen to Your Players' Problems

If you don't listen to your players' problems, they may make the natural assumption that you don't really care that much about them. If they simply don't bring their problems to you, it either means they

COUNSEL FROM THE COURT

Geno Auriemma, the outstanding women's basketball coach at the University of Connecticut, has been quoted as saying, "Nothing is more important than being hard on your best player." Is he implying that you have to yell at and criticize your best player constantly? Of course not! He's simply saying, "No double standards!" If you hold your best players to the highest expectations in terms of effort, commitment to team, and sportsmanship, then the players will quickly accept that everyone is accountable to a standard even more important than performance and winning: respect for self, teammates, and the sport.

feel that you don't care or they don't believe you can help them. Either way, you've failed as a leader. Anson Dorrance, women's soccer coach at the University of North Carolina, sums it up nicely when he says that women athletes won't care about what you have to say until they sense that you care.

Be approachable. You must be accessible and available. If a player is willing to come to you with a problem, it's because she needs guidance or reassurance. Your ability to help your players grow and become self-reliant is your most sacred charge as coach. Take whatever time is necessary.

Coaching Tips
During UC Davis's 1996–1997 run to the NCAA Division II Women's Final Four, our players often used "fun" to describe the key reason for our success. Some people thought we had fun because we were successful, but all members of that 29–3 squad know it was the other way around.

In addition, some coaches create an environment in which seeking help is perceived as a sign of weakness. This leads to the covering of mistakes and of finger-pointing to deflect blame, both of which do tremendous damage to the team. If a coach shows an appreciation for the efforts and challenges of his or her staff and players (even while setting high standards for them) and shows a willingness to admit mistakes, players are more likely to sense an empathetic perspective.

Pay Attention to the Details

This is all about preparation and anticipation. The better prepared you are, the more likely that strategies will be carried out efficiently. If you are disorganized, those around you will begin to have doubts. If this is a weak area for you, you need an assistant with this particular strength.

Conversely, being obsessive about a routine can get old in a hurry. Plus it tends to breed conformity and complacency. Routine will eventually trump creativity almost every time, and your team can lose its motivation.

Be a Flexible Leader

Every situation is different. Try to avoid rigidity in how you approach problems. One situation might lend itself to a team discussion, while another might be handled best with a concise directive.

Some aspects of the game require you to hover closely, while others call for a long leash. For example, defense is like playing the scales in music—it's very precise. Our players at UC Davis know exactly how to defend a baseline drive, which player helps on-ball, who rotates to strongside, where the secondary rotation comes from. They know this because we've drilled it over and over again in practice. If even one player misses her assignment, the entire system risks a breakdown. There is little room for deviation. As coach, you must demand strict adherence to your defensive "principles."

On the other hand, offense is like jazz—far more improvisational. Players are constantly "reading" the defense, making countless split-second decisions while on the move. You can't always decide ahead of time what you are going to do. If you try to control your players too much at the offensive end of the floor, you risk making them robotic and, thus, easy to defend.

Be an Optimist

Enthusiasm and optimism can achieve great things. They truly are infectious. This doesn't mean viewing blatant incompetence through rose-colored glasses. It means believing that the group *can* change

OFFENSE VERSUS DEFENSE

There's an old saying in basketball: "Offense sells tickets. Defense wins championships." The point? Offense, though exciting to watch, is less consistent than defense. Offense is touch, feel, and rhythm. Defense is hard work and effort. Even the most talented shooters have off games, when the ball just won't go through the basket. Good defense is consistent because it's predicated on effort, something players can give every game. So a team that plays strong defense will keep every game close, even when struggling to score, giving them an opportunity to win each time they step on the floor.

things for the better. Identify the problem and then, rather than focusing on what's wrong, emphasize how to make things better.

Keep in mind that encouraging does not necessarily mean *always* trying to please or make people happy. Which brings me to . . .

Being Responsible Means Irritating Some People from Time to Time

As coach, your responsibility is for the welfare of the group as well as the individuals. Trying to get everyone to like you is a mistake. Doing so means you'll avoid tough decisions and confrontations. You'll try to reward everyone the same so as not to upset people. In the end, you'll only upset your most dedicated players. In youth basketball, it's important to reward those who are trying to do the right thing, who set the right example and give maximum effort.

Surround Yourself with Good People

This is mentioned last, but it's the most critical aspect of leadership. Unless you want to spend the bulk of your coaching energies putting out brush fires, you need to surround yourself with the best people you can possibly find. In coaching youth basketball, your staff is likely to be made up of volunteers, like yourself. In other words, you may not be in a position to be choosy or too selective in putting together a staff. What do you look for in people? Intelligence and judgment, with emphasis on the latter. The two don't always go hand in hand. Integrity and loyalty are critical. Perhaps most important, look for enthusiasm. You're looking to motivate and inspire these young girls, and nothing does that better than playing for coaches who act like they really want to be there!

As coach, you will install a system that provides structure. But your "system" won't implement ideas. You and your staff will. Your players will. So attract, inspire, unleash.

Even with your staff and players, leadership can be lonely to some degree. The essence of leadership is the willingness to make tough, unambiguous choices and to stand by them. If you believe you are right, you can't flinch from this responsibility.

COACHING STYLE

Say the word "coach" to most people, and the image that pops to mind is a clipboard-wielding, whistle-wearing lunatic, screaming at some poor player who had the audacity to make a mistake while on his or her watch. A one-dimensional caricature? Sure, but one grounded in what used to be accepted as the coaching norm (*see* Knight, Bobby). Fortunately, those methods are rapidly vanishing, and the concept of coach as nurturer and educator is firmly taking hold. It may take Hollywood a while to catch up, but that's of no concern to us.

What *is* our concern is developing our own coaching philosophy and style (*philosophy* meaning what you want to accomplish as coach, and *style* meaning how you implement that philosophy). There is no template for determining your coaching style. Just be you. As mentioned earlier, young kids are very intuitive about people. If you try to be someone you are not, they will expose you quickly. Instead, be true to your personality, whether reserved or outgoing, and blend that with the key traits of enthusiasm, honesty, integrity, and consistency. Do this and you will be a blessing to all the young athletes who are fortunate enough to have you work with them.

Philosophy

When we talk about philosophy, we're really talking about two different things: (1) your values and teaching style and (2) your basketball system (X's and O's).

Values

Your players and their parents must gain a sense of what you stand for, what your expectations are, and what methods you will use to help the players and team achieve their goals. If the youngsters know what you expect of them, they will be more comfortable with the situation and more likely to adhere to your wishes. If you have team rules, spell them out clearly and define the consequences for any violations. Provide written copies for both players and their parents. (For more on team rules and discipline, see chapter 2.)

Meet with both players and parents and let them know what kind of time commitment you expect, what additional costs (if any) might be expected, and what your goals for the season are. Doing this can head off many potential misunderstandings. Be an active, rather than reactive, coach.

Basketball System

When it comes to actual basketball strategies and philosophy, most coaches draw from what's familiar. If you are an ex-player, initially you'll likely use a system similar to what you played in. From there, try to build your knowledge base through the many resources available to coaches nowadays (see the "Coaching Resources" sidebar and the appendix). Another great way to learn is to find a more experienced coach who is willing to help mentor you. Each season, young coaches who are coaching their first team approach me for advice on practice planning, drills, or offenses and defenses. Most coaches love to exchange ideas and "talk basketball" when time allows. Take a coach out for pizza and in no time at all salt and pepper shakers will become "players," napkin dispensers will represent "baskets," and you'll have a "court" outlined in straws! It's a great way to learn!

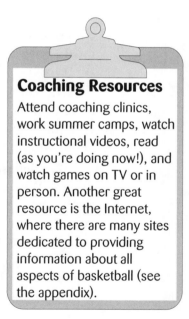

Coaching Resources

Attend coaching clinics, work summer camps, watch instructional videos, read (as you're doing now!), and watch games on TV or in person. Another great resource is the Internet, where there are many sites dedicated to providing information about all aspects of basketball (see the appendix).

If you are coaching a youth team, chances are you don't need (or want) a very sophisticated offensive and defensive system. Keeping it simple is always a good idea, especially with young players. Still, there is always a "better" way to teach this skill or to run that drill. A good coach is constantly searching for that better way. Talking with other coaches is one of the best ways to achieve that.

Keep in mind that your players will, to a large degree, dictate a preferred style of play. If you have a large, ponderous squad, you may not want to emphasize a fastbreak style of play. Conversely, if your team is small, but quick, you may want to employ a full-court pressure defense to mitigate the size advantage most teams will have against you. At the college level, you can recruit a certain type of athlete to fit your system. In youth basketball, you may need to adapt your system every year to utilize your available talent. Even then, the emphasis should be on teaching fundamental skills and teamwork as opposed to employing a complicated team system.

KEYS TO SUCCESSFUL COACHING

While each coach must be true to his or her personality to be an effective leader and teacher, their are some traits commonly found in most successful coaches. Here are six characteristics of most successful teachers:

1.   Enthusiasm. It *is* infectious, you know. You don't necessarily have to be a rah-rah–style leader. But your players will detect soon enough whether you enjoy what you're doing. If you are excited about working with them, they will respond in kind.

2.   Honesty. This is an absolute must, but employ it with velvet gloves. When offering evaluations or giving feedback, it's best to avoid the brutal form of honesty that may prove insensitive and counterproductive. While you want to avoid "sugarcoating" all of your remarks, you may wish to couch your constructive comments in positive tones, praising, for example, her great effort before attempting to correct the skill involved.

3.   Consistency. Most athletes, especially young ones, can be happy playing under almost any coaching style if they know what to expect from the coach and what is expected of them.

4.   Humor. Allow for some laughter at practice. It's a sign that the players are having fun, which is a good thing. Just because some of your players are giggling, it doesn't necessarily mean there is a lack of discipline.

5. Integrity. Set the example. Your responsibility is to help develop your athletes as people as well as players. Coaching is no place for a "Do as I say, not as I do" approach.

6. Organization. Nearly all successful coaches are well organized. This probably applies even more to coaching in practices than in games. Think ahead, anticipate, and have a plan.

YOUR RESPONSIBILITIES AS A COACH

Time Commitment

The level of time commitment required by coaching varies widely depending on the age level and structure of the program. But, with the exception of the highest echelon in the coaching profession (top-level Division I universities and the professional ranks), you need to understand this: You will never be paid adequately for the hours you put in. And you shouldn't care! If you're in it for the money, it's time to get out.

The number of hours you need to commit to should be whatever it takes to do right by your athletes. At the youth sport level, your commitment will likely be limited to organizing and conducting practices as well as games. There may be some travel involved and, in some cases, occasional fundraising responsibilities, but in general you're looking at no more than a few hours per week. And since you are probably volunteering your time, that's all it should require.

Coaching middle school or high school teams is another matter. Though you'll usually receive a small stipend, it will end up working out to about $1.35 an hour (if that!) over the course of the season. Again, you are coaching because you love it and because you enjoy working with children. And you can't put a dollar figure on that.

Liability

One of your primary responsibilities as a coach is to provide for the safety of your athletes. While almost all youth sport organizations require parents to sign "consent forms" that detail the inherent risks of participating in a particular sport, all the paperwork in the world won't stop litigious parents from suing over an injury to their daughter. And the most likely strategy behind such a suit will focus on either improper skill instruction or an unsafe physical environment. It is a good idea for any coach to carry an insurance rider increasing personal liability coverage. Such coverage is relatively inexpensive and, while likely never to be necessary, provides a certain peace of mind.

Providing Skill Instruction

Whether or not the way a coach teaches a certain skill is "safe" is a subjective matter, making this area all too vulnerable for a lawyer hoping to prove negligence. To safeguard yourself to the greatest extent possible, you should follow these general guidelines:

- Teach within the rules of the game. In other words, don't teach skills that violate the rules of basketball. A very few coaches teach skills that provide an "advantage" for a player who "gets away" with the illegal maneuver. This is not only unethical and teaches the wrong values, it also opens up the coach to charges of negligence if an athlete is injured in the process. Play by the rules and the "inherent risk" standard becomes a coach's ally.

- Don't conduct drills that involve contact in excess of the game's norm. Drills that encourage play of an overly physical nature invite trouble. A good example would be setting up a "take the charge" drill (not a good idea, in my estimation, under any circumstances) where the coach encourages the offensive player to "run over" the defender.

Creating a Safe Environment

Creating a safe practice and playing environment for your team need not be a complex process. Most gym facilities are fairly standard in their construct. But there are some basic things to keep in mind:

- Sweep the floor prior to practice. Most gyms serve multipurpose uses, and the floor can quickly build up a thin layer of dust over the course of the day. Basketball requires a lot of cutting and change-of-direction movements. If the floor is slippery, there is an obvious increased risk of injury. If dry mopping the floor doesn't appreciably improve footing, you may wish to consider placing some damp towels around the dry mop before sweeping the floor. Make sure you allow for adequate drying time before your players take the floor.

- Make certain that there is padding on the basket supports (if they are portable or freestanding bases) and on the walls behind the basket if they are close to the baseline.

- Move loose equipment (volleyball or badminton standards and nets, equipment cages, PE equipment) to corners and well out of harm's way to a hustling player chasing down a loose ball.

- Never leave any young person, but especially a young girl, who may be waiting for a ride from a parent or friend, unattended at the gym following a practice or game. Make sure all of your athletes are safely on their way before locking up and leaving.

Injury Prevention

Injuries are a part of any athletic endeavor, and while it's probably unrealistic to expect a totally injury-free season, there are steps you can take to help avoid placing your players at any more risk than necessary. In addition to the equipment and facilities issues already addressed, the steps you can take include:

- **Preseason physical exam and consent form.** This is usually a youth league or school requirement for participation. The physical exam helps ensure that each participant is of sufficient health to participate, and the consent form outlines the inherent risks of the activity and provides permission for emergency medical treatment in the event of an injury. More and more organizations are now requesting complete health insurance coverage information as well.

- **Physical conditioning program.** One of the best methods of injury prevention is a strong, well-conditioned body. Preworkout stretching is one component of this program. While most young children are extremely flexible and can probably get by without stretching much, a thorough warm-up routine is a good habit to instill. See chapter 5 for more detailed information on conditioning and stretching regimens.

- **Proper supervision.** All activities should be closely supervised. Just being present in the gym may not be enough. Kids are notoriously squirrelly, and it doesn't take long for a drill you have initiated to escalate to roughhousing or other shenanigans, increasing the risk of injury.

- **Good records.** Have accident report forms on site and fill them out in as much detail as possible should an injury occur. Keep a copy of all your practice plans as well, as evidence that you have been providing the proper foundation for your players.

- **Water breaks.** This sounds obvious, but there are still some old-school coaches who parcel out water breaks sparingly under the guise of building toughness. Hydration is an absolute key, for both safety and performance. Provide frequent water breaks for your players.

Injury Treatment

Coaching Tip

For ankle sprains, think ICE:

- **Ice** the area to prevent swelling and to help reduce pain.

- **Compress** the injured area securely with an elastic wrap of some sort.

- **Elevate** the injured ankle in order to keep blood flow to the affected area to a minimum.

No matter how thorough you are in trying to prevent injuries, they will occur. Basketball is one of the top four injury-producing youth sports (partly because of the high rate of player participation). Most injuries are not severe enough to limit playing, but they may require some medical attention on your part. Make sure you have a basic first-aid kit on-site for any practice or game.

For minor cuts and abrasions, the first thing to do is don a pair of disposable surgical gloves. Avoid direct contact with the blood. Make an effort to stop the bleeding, then clean out the wound. Finally, dress the cut with gauze or some form of bandage.

In the event of a serious injury, immediately call for emergency medical assistance (always have a cell phone available). Remain with the injured athlete until EMTs have arrived. Perform assisted breathing or cardiopulmonary resuscitation (CPR) as necessary.

COACHING YOUR OWN DAUGHTER

Quite often, the volunteer coach of a youth team is a well-intentioned parent. If you are in the position of coaching your daughter, there are a few things to consider as you ponder the dual role of parent/coach:

- Ask your daughter if she wants you to coach her team.
- Discuss with your daughter how your interaction may be different at practice and games than it is at home.
- Don't be a parent at practice.
- Don't be a coach at home.
- Treat your daughter fairly. Don't fall into the trap of treating her more severely in order to evade charges of favoritism.

Coaching your child can be a rich and rewarding experience for the both of you as long as the coach and parent roles are clearly delineated. Make sure you let her know often how much you love her, regardless of her athletic performance.

2

STRATEGIES FOR COACHING THE YOUNG FEMALE ATHLETE

NOW THAT YOU'VE carefully considered the time commitment and responsibilities that accompany coaching and have looked at the personal qualities that will help you be a successful coach, it's time to take reins in hand. It is your job to bring a group of young girls together, develop their individual basketball skills, and show them that being part of a team is a remarkable experience.

But how do you go about doing this? Remember that earlier I encouraged you to view the role of a coach as educator. Well, that is all that coaching really is . . . teaching. And as any good teacher knows, the trinity of effective learning is communication, motivation, and discipline. This chapter examines each of these three components and looks at how you, as coach, can maximize your efficiency as a teacher by giving proper attention to each.

EFFECTIVE COMMUNICATION

Communicating with Players

Communication is not simply a matter of giving instruction on how to perform a skill or how to play the game. You will use verbal commands extensively, yet they will still comprise only a fraction of

Coaching Tip

It's not just *what* you say, but *how* you say it. Body language speaks volumes. Folding your arms across your chest and furrowing your brow will make you appear unapproachable or upset. A gentle smile accompanying constructive feedback will be reassuring to the player who is looking to learn.

what you will communicate to your players over the course of a practice or during a game. A large portion of your communication will be nonverbal, through body language and facial expressions. Children have an innate ability to pick up the subtlest of nonverbal cues, and it's important to be aware of how you come across.

Also, young athletes are often unsure of themselves and may lack confidence in their ability to play basketball. It is vitally important to be as positive as possible when communicating (again, verbally *and* nonverbally) with young players. Emphasize the things they are doing well and be sensitive to every child's need for positive reinforcement.

When you communicate with your athletes, whether it be praise or constructive feedback, keep the following five guidelines in mind:

1. Be positive.
2. Be objective, not subjective.
3. Keep it simple.
4. Be consistent.
5. Listen.

Be Positive

There is *nothing* more important than giving positive feedback to your young players. When one of your players does something well, offer her praise. If players hear from you only when they've made a mistake, they will come to dread the sound of your voice and will eventually tune you out. You can certainly correct performance mistakes, but couch your feedback in terms that emphasize the positive aspects of her effort. This will convey your sense of confidence that she will get it right the next time.

Save your scolding and punitive measures for problems of misbehavior or poor attitude. If one of your players is not paying attention, is acting inappropriately, or is generally being a thorn in your side, by all means remove her from the activity and let her know of your disapproval. But, if you're addressing a performance issue, stay positive and encouraging. Remember that no one, especially kids, tries to play poorly. They're learning, and they're going to make mistakes.

Your body language and facial expressions can send strong messages as well. Disgust, irritation, and impatience are all easily expressed via nonverbal means, and, believe me, the kids notice. All eyes routinely zero in on the coach when someone makes a mistake. How you react to those mistakes will go a long way toward determining your effectiveness as a coach. A smile can be very reassuring to your players, allowing them to relax and perform their best.

One last form of nonverbal communication that can be very effective is physical contact. Giving a high-five, a pat on the head, or an arm around the shoulder can express approval, affection, and enthusiasm. Understand that some young children may not be

COUNSEL FROM THE COURT

Years ago, I coached a young girl who obviously suffered from low self-esteem. No matter how hard the coaching staff tried to build her confidence and to point out the positive things she did as a player, she always focused on the negative. One day, after practice, I wrote her a long note by hand, telling her how far she had progressed as a player, the confidence I had in her abilities, and my firm belief that, with continued hard work in certain areas, she would be a great player someday. I was quite pleased with myself when I was done.

Imagine my surprise the next evening when I received a phone call from the young girl's parents. Did she read and appreciate my compliments? Was she pleased with my demonstration of confidence in her? Was she motivated to apply herself like never before? No, no, and no. Her sole reaction was that I was so anxious to sit down and tell her how terrible a player she was (remember the part about "continued hard work in certain areas"?) that I couldn't bother waiting to get to a computer to type it all out!

Granted her reaction was extreme, but it taught me a lesson that remains one of my strongest convictions: When offering feedback, make sure that your player understands that you may occasionally criticize what she *does*, but never who she *is*.

comfortable with any kind of physical contact (be particularly sensitive if you are a male coach working with young female athletes); if you have any sense that this is the case, do not press the issue. Instead, give them some room. Obviously, any form of physical contact should be appropriate and nonintrusive. But appropriate physical contact can be a tremendously positive reinforcer for young children.

Be Objective, Not Subjective

One of the biggest differences between male and female athletes is that girls, while intrinsically more receptive to instruction and feedback than boys, are also more likely to personalize criticism than are their male counterparts. In other words, when you correct a young girl, she is more likely to hear you criticizing *who she is*, rather than *what she did*. If you tell Samantha that she needs to maintain better contact when blocking out on the boards, she is quite likely to process that as "Coach doesn't like me."

Coaching Tip

One of the key elements in learning a physical skill is repetition. The same goes for your verbal instructions. Say the same thing in different ways. If you want your players to "force the ball to the baseline," on defense, express that to them. A littler later, say, "Let's take away the drive to the middle."

Keep It Simple

Express yourself in concise, easy-to-understand statements. Rambling leads to inattention and confusion over what the main point or emphasis may be. Be thorough, but not long-winded. Don't speak down to your players: They're young but intelligent. Allow them to ask questions and to clarify the points you've made.

Be Consistent

Sending mixed messages is never constructive. Make sure that your athletes can count on your philosophy to remain consistent. They will adjust to your expectations and improve performance. If you are constantly contradicting yourself, you will confuse your team.

Listen

This is perhaps the most crucial element of communication. Listen to your players. If you take the time to talk with your players, stay with the moment. Give your complete attention to them and stay focused on what they're saying, as well as on what they are *not* saying. If you truly listen to your players, they will believe that you care and that, in turn, will go a long way in gaining their trust.

Practice dialogue, not monologue. Even young children have something to say, and their refreshing honesty can be a valuable resource in helping you become a better coach. Let your young athletes ask "Why?" occasionally. Don't interpret that question as a challenge to your authority. It's a question you should be able to answer. If not, then it may be time to re-examine exactly that: Why *are* you doing something a specific way?

Communicating with Parents

Being a youth coach involves more than just interacting and communicating with your players. How successfully you communicate with your players' parents will go a long way in determining how enjoyable the coaching experience will be for you. Parents need to feel that their daughter is playing for a coach who is both knowledgeable and caring. If parents are given the sense that you have their daughter's best interests at heart, they will likely be supportive and positive throughout the season.

Conflict is unavoidable in the coaching profession. Accept this: *Every* parent knows more than you do about the game, the disparity growing in inverse proportion to how much playing time their daughter receives. Some parents are more prone than others to sharing their suggestions with you, but the fact remains that you will be second-guessed constantly. It comes with the territory, and, honestly, most criticism is fairly benign. Nothing disrespectful is really meant. Learn to roll with the comments, and you will be happier for it.

But you can head off many potential conflicts by communicating proactively. Many misunderstandings are simply the result of miscommunication. Here are a few things to consider:

Call a Parents' Meeting

Holding a parents' meeting early in the season is a great way to start. Use this orientation session to communicate your expectations and philosophy to all of the parents. Make attendance mandatory (at least one parent) for their daughter's participation. At this meeting, you should clearly describe your background qualifications and describe precisely what your goals are for the team and players. For example, if you will be coaching a team of 7- and 8-year-olds and you will be stressing participation over competition, be clear about that. On the other hand, if you are coaching a squad of 13-year-olds and feel that winning is of a higher priority, make sure the parents understand that not every player will get equal playing time.

The orientation meeting is also an excellent time to solicit volunteers to help transport the team, assist in fundraisers, and provide postgame snacks or drinks, if you wish to have parents involved. The more parents are involved within the enterprise, the more vested they'll feel and the more positive they'll remain.

Give parents an opportunity to ask questions and raise any concerns they may have. Really make an effort to listen, and try to offer positive responses to all issues. You may not always be on the same page with every parent, but it is important to keep the lines of communication open. We all want our voices to be heard. If you make an effort to listen, your parents will likely support you even when there is mild disagreement.

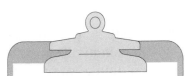

Coaching Tip

If you have policies regarding tardiness, player behavior, or attendance at practice as conditions of game participation, clearly designate them and present them to parents in writing, along with any resulting consequences. Have parents sign two copies and keep one for themselves.

Make a Team Calendar

Today's families are constantly on the go, juggling commitments and trying to coordinate family members' busy schedules. One of the best ways to assure that your players' families keep track of your team's schedule is to provide a calendar that lists every practice, game, meeting, and ancillary activity. Merely putting together a list of dates and providing it to parents may not be good enough. Lists tend to disappear, while calendars may find their rightful place on the family bulletin board. With today's calendar software programs, compiling one is a snap. Provide copies to your parents at the orientation meeting. Copies sent home through your players have a tendency to become lost or forgotten.

Work with Angry Parents

If you coach long enough, you will be forced to deal with a parent who is upset about some aspect of your coaching. Parents can express their displeasure in many different ways, but when confronted by a parent who is upset, say, about how much his or her daughter is playing in games, try to remain calm and resist getting defensive. Stay firm in your convictions, but understand that he loves his daughter and wants her to be happy. As long as parents express themselves in an appropriate manner, hear them out and try to be positive in response. If parents seem too emotional, suggest to them that you would be happy to discuss their concerns at a later time, after they have had an opportunity to calm down. You will not be able to placate every upset parent you encounter, however. Sometimes you must just agree to disagree.

Coaching Tip

Set boundaries for parents about when you are available for discussion. Clearly communicate to parents if you don't wish to be called at home or if you wish to set an evening curfew for phone calls. Just don't make the boundaries too prohibitive!

Most important, don't hold a girl's parents against her. Just because a mom or dad is complaining about a decision of yours, it doesn't necessarily mean that the daughter agrees. Kids are very resilient and adaptable. Your players are probably having a great experience, meeting new friends, developing their skills, and enjoying the game. Most players would be mortified by the thought of their parents complaining to their coach. So don't let any difference of opinion with a parent affect how you treat their daughter, the player. The girl is probably as happy as a bounce-passing clam.

EFFECTIVE TEACHING

No matter how much basketball you may know, it will be useless knowledge unless you have the ability to teach it to others. Being an effective teacher involves patience and a positive attitude. It also requires organization and the ability to teach physical skills. Let's take a look at what's necessary for teaching basketball skills.

Organization

Know *what* you want to do and *how* you want to accomplish it before setting foot on the practice floor. Winging it is never a good idea. You will end up confusing yourself and your players. Think through how you want to teach any given skill, the points you wish to emphasize, and the progressions you want to use. This will enable you to make maximum use of your practice time.

Skill Instruction

Coaching youth basketball involves spending a great deal of time teaching fundamental individual skills. If you can equip your young players with these basic skills, it will make learning the team aspect of the game easier and far more enjoyable. Here are some steps that will make teaching physical skills more effective:

1. **Explain.** When introducing a skill for the first few times, it is important not only to explain *what* the skill is, but also to explain *why* it's important. Young athletes need to know why they're learning something. For example, when teaching pivoting, you can inform them that the pivot is an important component of all individual offensive play. So, before they can learn any one-on-one offensive moves, they'll need to know how to pivot correctly.

2. **Demonstrate.** Some of us are verbal learners and some are visual learners. But when it comes to learning a physical skill, nearly all of us learn more quickly if the skill is demonstrated. If you cannot effectively perform the skill, find someone (an assistant coach or possibly one of your players) who can perform it and use her for the

demonstration. Demonstrate the skill several times. Some of the repetitions should be in slow motion, emphasizing specific techniques. Talk your players through each step of the demonstration.

3. Practice. Have your players perform the new skill. Some athletes may have to be physically guided through their first few attempts. Be patient and offer praise for trying. Let them know it's okay to make mistakes, especially when trying something new . . . it's how we learn. I tell athletes at every level that if they never fail, they're never testing their limits.

Patience is the key to teaching physical skills. While some young girls will pick up a new skill quickly, most will need time and many repetitions. Some children become easily frustrated if they experience frequent failure. Staying positive is crucial for these kids. Reassure them that they're getting better with each try and offer generous praise for even incremental improvements.

Coaching Tip
Young children have notoriously short attention spans. So keep the talking to a minimum and keep them as active as possible. Don't spend too long (more than 10 minutes) on any given activity.

EFFECTIVE MOTIVATION

Longtime NBA coach Pat Riley once said, "It's not my job to motivate my players, it's their job to motivate me." He is wrong, of course. A good portion of a coach's job is to motivate players, and the team as a whole, to perform at the highest level they are capable of.

When many people think of "motivation" in sport, they envision a dramatic, inspirational speech by the coach designed to raise players' emotions to a peak level just prior to a contest. True motivation, however, is really about creating an environment where your players *want* to learn and *want* to play. Female athletes draw much of their motivation from the level of team chemistry (relationships are very important to them) and from their self-perception as athletes. Since most girls view themselves more negatively than their male

OFFER HER AN OREO COOKIE

One of the most effective ways to correct skill performance mistakes is to demonstrate the correct form for the player (chocolate cookie), then show the player what *they* did (cream filling), followed by another demonstration of correct skill execution (chocolate cookie, again!). Always accompany your demonstration with positive comments about something the athlete did well during her attempt.

counterparts do, it is important to look for opportunities to genuinely build their esteem.

Cultivating an environment of individual self-esteem and positive team chemistry can go a long way toward motivating your players. Manage to do both and you will be faced each practice or game with a gaggle of happy athletes who look forward to the challenge of improving themselves and the team.

EFFECTIVE TEAM DISCIPLINE

First off, if you, in any way, associate discipline with punishment, discard that perspective right now. The latter doesn't establish the former. For older athletes, I've always interpreted discipline to mean poise in the face of pressure or adversity. For younger athletes, "discipline" is really just another word for "structure." Kids need it, and it's your job as coach to provide it.

Rules

In constructing your team guidelines, establish only enforceable rules, and then be consistent about their application. Any rules you have apply to all—players, parents, and coaches. If you play favorites or appear to have a double standard, you will lose your players and their parents. Your credibility will be brought into question.

Don't have too many rules. Your intent should be to guide, not control. And don't make a rule that you cannot enforce. However, once you establish a rule, stick with it and faithfully carry out the consequences for violations.

Expectations

Make sure your players understand what your behavioral expectations of them are. Courtesy and respect should be at the forefront. Also, let them know it's okay to make mistakes, but you expect them to always try their best.

Punishment

Remember, do not punish performance, only behavior. For example, if one of your players misses a lay-up or makes a bad pass, it is not cause for punishment. After all, she wasn't *trying* to miss the shot or throw the ball away. But if that same player throws a ball at a teammate in anger or curses in frustration, it might be cause for punitive measures.

If you do punish a player, remain calm while doing so. Don't make it personal. And let completion of the penance be the end of it. Whether you asked the player to sit off to the side or whether you made her run, when she is done serving her "sentence," it's done, over with. Do not continue to punish her by treating her differently from the other players.

RUNNING AS PUNISHMENT

If you must use running as a form of punishment, be careful how you do so. Any running that you employ as punishment will gain a negative association in your players' minds. Since you may also like to use certain running drills as a method of physical conditioning, you don't want to use one of those punitively. Otherwise, your athletes will come to see conditioning time in negative terms. You may want to select a particular running drill as one you would use, for punishment and only sparingly.

BEING A ROLE MODEL

In the end, all of your rules and words will mean little if your athletes are unable to hold you up as a role model to emulate. By staying positive in the face of adversity, by treating everyone with whom you come in contact with courtesy and respect, and by demonstrating every day, through your actions, that you are committed to the welfare of each of your players, you will establish yourself as someone your young athletes can look up to. And years after they've left your care, they will remember you fondly, while cherishing the opportunity they had to play for a coach who helped guide them in the right direction.

COACHING GIRLS VERSUS BOYS

KIDS TODAY ARE subject to a host of influences that shape them as they grow. Children are defined by family values, peer influence, and media images as they develop physically, psychologically, and emotionally. As a youth coach, it is important for you to be sensitive to the various factors that help shape who your young athletes are and who they will become. By understanding the underlying influences, you will be better able to relate to your players on an appropriate developmental level and increase your chances of creating a positive, fulfilling, and fun environment.

HOW GIRLS PLAY VERSUS BOYS

Do boys and girls generally play differently? Yes. But in denoting those differences, we can easily make the mistake of overlooking all the similarities. That being said, research has shown that substantive differences do exist between how girls and boys approach physical activity, including sports. The differences do not appear to be grounded in genetics, but in socialization.

Boys and girls often have different early childhood experiences of physical play. Many parents, especially dads, play differently (and less frequently) with their daughters than they do with their sons.

PHYSICALITY: NATURE OR NURTURE?

While research has demonstrated that many fathers play differently with their sons than they do with their daughters, I do not count myself among them. My wife constantly points out that she and I have "different" relationships with our 4-year-old daughter. And it's true. Daddy is the parent our Olivia comes to when she wants to roughhouse or get tossed around. I have played that role for her since infancy, and she has grown up to be a fairly physical child in terms of coordination and athletic interests. Was she born to be a physical athlete, and that's why she invites me to wrestle and toss? Or is she interested in sports because of how I've played with her since infancy?

Father-son play is generally more physically active than is father-daughter play. As a result, the messages boys receive about physical activity vary from those that girls receive.

Because of these messages, youngsters usually have a clear (if not always accurate) idea of their physical skills. Even though skill levels in most physical activities are about the same at the youngest ages, boys see themselves as being physically skilled more often than do girls. According to sport sociologist Cynthia Hasbrook, this results in higher self-confidence for boys and a greater willingness to test their limits. A vicious cycle ensues. Boys more often exhibit physical prowess, and our society treats it as *superiority,* as opposed to the more accurate *opportunity.* Go watch almost any grade-school recess, and you'll see "boys'" games spread out and dominating the landscape. Most girls will be off to the sides playing less physically aggressive games. It has less to do with ability than it does expectation and opportunity.

PHYSICAL DIFFERENCES BETWEEN BOYS AND GIRLS

Size and Strength

There is a pervading belief that girls mature physically faster than do boys through childhood and pre-adolescence. This is due to the fact that girls develop physically at a more or less linear rate, maintaining a steady rate of growth up through about age 15. Boys, on the other hand, physically mature at a linear rate until age 13–14, *then* they experience a growth spurt in both size and strength. The result is that they appear to mature later. The flip side of this phenomenon is that girls and boys are on fairly equal footing until about age 13.

The most significant difference in strength ratio in boys and girls is in the upper body. Until age 10 or so, boys and girls have similar elbow and arm strength. After that, boys' strength can increase significantly, while girls' improvement remains steady and linear. Lower-body strength remains largely equal between genders throughout physical development to full maturity.

In other words, young female athletes are every bit as capable and strong in the legs and torso as are their male peers. Their elbow and arm strength is also largely comparable until age 12–13. Where boys seem to have a strength advantage throughout is in the shoulder and upper back areas. Still, in the younger athlete, size and strength differences are negligible until adolescence.

Menstruation

Young female athletes commence menstruating at a later age than do non-athletes. The average age of menarche in healthy North American girls is generally between the ages of 12 and 13. For athletes across a wide variety of sports, the average age at onset is one to two years later. Some have expressed concern that training for sports results in a delay of menstruation. Low caloric intake, low body fat, and the stress of training and competition have all been cited as possible factors. Still, no definitive study has been able to draw a correlation. It is quite possible that girls who possess some of the physical characteristics that can be an advantage in many sports (narrow hips, lean body mass, and slender physiques) are more likely to begin menstruating later regardless of their involvement in sports.

Of greater concern to you as a coach of young girls is not so much the onset of the menstrual cycle, but its regularity. Amenorrhea, or cessation of menstrual cycles after menarche, can occur due to intense physical training. Several studies have suggested that maintenance of less than 17–20 percent body fat can put young women at risk of amenorrhea. If it lasts for too long, amenorrhea can cause a decrease in bone density, making the young athlete a candidate for stress fractures in the short term and osteoporosis in the long view. It may also be a red flag, alerting you, because of its connection to body-fat percentage, to the possibility of an eating disorder (see later in this chapter). If you have an athlete you know is experiencing significant irregularities with, or cessation of, her menstrual cycle, you may need to communicate tactfully with her parents and encourage them to consult a physician. It may be time to re-examine the girl's nutritional program to increase caloric intake and cut back on her physical training to help her regain her cycle.

PSYCHOLOGICAL DIFFERENCES BETWEEN BOYS AND GIRLS

Why They Play

I mentioned in the introduction to this book that most children, boys and girls, become involved in youth sports with the intention of having *fun*. In fact, a 1991 *USA Today* poll revealed that 88 percent of the youth sport respondents said "fun" was the overriding reason for playing. In addition, making new friends and maintaining existing friendships also ranked high on their list of priorities. The response placing a distant fourth was the desire to develop their skills in a particular sport.

Contrasting those reasons for participating are the reasons for dropping out of youth sports. A 1991 study by Michigan State University's Youth Sports Institute concluded that some of the top reasons for young girls' discontinuing participation were: no longer interested, it was no longer fun, coach was a poor teacher, and too much pressure. Pressure, of course, can come in myriad forms, but the general trend is that the "pressure" cited referred to the emphasis on performance and winning and came mostly from parents and coaches.

It is a good idea to keep separate in your mind the *benefits* of playing youth sports and the *reasons* children give for playing. Think of the benefits (development of teamwork, cooperation, and following rules; allowing children to explore their bodies' capabilities and

WHY GIRLS DO AND DON'T PLAY

Here are the primary reasons that girls get involved with, and drop out of, organized youth sports:

TOP FOUR REASONS GIRLS PLAY

1. It's fun!
2. Peers (friends) are playing.
3. They want to make new friends.
4. They want to develop skills.

TOP FOUR REASONS GIRLS DROP OUT

1. They're no longer interested.
2. It's no longer fun.
3. There's too much pressure.
4. Coach was a poor teacher.

limitations) as tangential to the experience of playing a sport. They are some of the positives of participation, but they are not *why* the child chooses to play in the first place. If you, as the coach, keep the fun and friendship factors constantly in mind, you are much more likely to create a positive environment for your young charges. Still, there are some differences, even at younger ages, between male and female athletes.

What They Value

The differences in the manner boys and girls approach sports are likely both a function of biology and socialization. The degree to which each influences behavior, however, is a question beyond the scope of this book. Research has demonstrated that the primary difference between boys' and girls' perspectives on sport is that boys value a hierarchical social order while girls value relationships.

Young boys define themselves and improve self-esteem by moving up in the social order of the team. The higher the skill and achievement level, the higher up the social ladder they are placed. Accomplishment and performance helps the male athlete differentiate himself from the group, and that independence is valued for the self-esteem it creates.

Pre-adolescent girls, on the other hand, are anchored in relationships. According to Carol Gilligan in her book *In a Different Voice,* interconnectedness is valued so strongly that hierarchical orders are rejected in favor of a paradigm that might best be called a web. The relationship web is one in which each athlete is connected to the others in a complicated pattern of mutual dependence. To be singled out from the group is to be on the periphery of the web, a position that makes most female athletes uncomfortable.

In general, then:

BOYS VALUE:
- Independence
- Status
- Achievement

GIRLS VALUE:
- Belonging
- Connectedness
- Friendships

BOYS FEAR:
- Failure
- Dependency
- Conformity

GIRLS FEAR:
- Isolation
- Separation
- Loneliness

WHAT ABOUT TOMBOYS?

While my observations are purely anecdotal, it has been my experience that "tomboys" (young girls who socialize and play with boys to a greater degree than they play with female peers) do not fall so neatly within the generalized male/female dichotomy. Their values and fears are often much closer to those of the average young boy in that their self-esteem and satisfaction levels are correlated more with skill level and achievement than with friendships and connectedness. This may be due to the strong socialization influences of growing up in a more male-influenced subculture of sports. Young girls whose dads frequently shoot baskets with them and allow them to play pick-up ball at the park on Saturday afternoons are going to participate in a different way than the young girl whose parents are overprotective or keep her close to home most of the time. And think about this: A Women's Sports Foundation survey of female executives at Fortune 500 companies found that 80 percent referred to themselves as "tomboys" in their youth.

One of the best things about coaching female athletes is that, given their concern with belonging and relationships, they are sensitive to their relationship with their coach and usually make stronger efforts to follow direction and to please. The flip side is that girls tend to personalize criticism to a greater degree than do their male counterparts. It is one of the most important gender differences to be aware of if you are going to coach young girls. You may think that you are motivating a player to get better by offering constructive feedback on her performance and what she needs to do better. But all she may be hearing is, "You don't like me!"

So couch your feedback in terms of what players can do to make the *team* better. Players may not necessarily care about becoming better individually, because that may mean becoming the best. This would marginalize their status among the team or move them further from the social web described earlier. If you can convince them that by working harder and improving their skills they will help make their *teammates* and *team* better, they will be much more receptive.

According to Gilligan, the differences in values and fears can be summed up as the male having "the wish to be alone at the top and the consequent fear that others will get too close" while the female athlete has "the wish to be at the center of the connection and the consequent fear of being too far out on the edge" (of the web). As with all

THREE KEYS TO GIVING FEEDBACK

1. **Avoid using a raised voice or sarcasm.** While raising your voice may be appropriate at times (particularly when addressing negative *behavior*), constructive feedback of performance should be done in an even-toned manner. Yelling simply refocuses your athlete's attention on the perceived breach in her relationship with you, and that distraction minimizes the reception of your feedback. Sarcasm works in much the same way.

2. **Keep it simple.** Many athletes become a bit anxious when a coach begins to address them. So, in addition to keeping a calm tone, keep your feedback objective and succinct. Don't ask your athletes to process too much at one time. If they have many areas to correct, dole out your feedback over time.

3. **As mentioned earlier, offer them an Oreo cookie.** When correcting a skill, demonstrate to them the correct technique, then show them how they performed the skill, then finish with a repetition of the correct method. A variation on this is to praise them for something *specific* they've been doing well, then correct the flawed skill, and finish up with a reaffirmation of what they have been doing correctly.

generalizations, it is understood that these values cross gender lines. Boys value friendships and belonging just as girls want to succeed and value a level of independence. In the end, we should be careful about perpetuating *differences* just because they exist. Rather we should strive to provide equitable athletic *opportunities* and *experiences* for both boys *and* girls.

Take the time to talk to your athletes and listen to *why* they play. Don't bring preconceived notions to your discussions. Understanding *what* it is that girls value in their sports experience is the first step. Use that knowledge to help provide a positive and fulfilling experience for each of your players. Not everyone will be motivated by the same things, because each athlete is unique.

SERIOUS ISSUES IN THE SPORT TODAY

Eating Disorders

Eating disorders, primarily anorexia nervosa and bulimia, are increasingly common among females. For certain female athletes, eating disorders have become a particularly acute problem. Though uncommon before the age of 12, the roots of the disorder (understand that this is a *mental health* issue with physical consequences) are likely to manifest themselves at younger ages. The key element is body image, or how the young female athlete perceives and values her physical appearance. In a society that constantly bombards women of all ages with the feminine "ideal" of slimness equaling attractiveness, it's little wonder that conflict over body image is rampant.

One NCAA study estimated that 58 percent of female athletes participating in gymnastics, distance running, swimming, and diving were at risk of developing eating disorders. The study referred to college-aged athletes, but as a youth sport coach, you need to be aware that your players are subject to the same social pressures as are older athletes. Here are some things to look for in identifying a young athlete potentially at risk:

- Athlete expresses a fear of gaining weight or becoming fat. She may also make constant references to how "fat" she is, even if she is obviously underweight.
- She displays "perfectionist" tendencies and is routinely hypercritical of her performances.
- She displays an obsessive interest in nutrition and caloric content of food.
- She exercises compulsively. If you learn that the player is going for runs or participating in extra cardiovascular routines, even after tough workouts, there may be some issues developing.

BODY IMAGE

Body image is, by its very definition, a psychosocial construct. Based on a synthesis of several studies, here are some aspects of body imaging:

1. Body images are psychological phenomena, not physical constructs.
2. Body images influence our behavior. Our perceptions fuel our actions.
3. Body image is personal and subjective. How we perceive ourselves may be very different from how others see us.
4. Body image is constantly changing. Perceptions shift with current circumstances.

The presence of any of these factors does not mean the young athlete has an eating disorder. But they are signs to be taken seriously. And never, *never* mention weight to a female athlete. Instead, talk of lean body mass.

Eating disorders are insidious in that the victims are often oblivious to their condition. Many see themselves as "health conscious" rather than as behaving abnormally. Even those who suspect they may have an issue are often unwilling to admit to a problem. And they are quite savvy, knowing exactly what to say to all inquiries. Efforts to help are often rebuffed. Trying to help a victim of anorexia nervosa or bulimia is a job for experts. Have your antennae up for at-risk behavior, but don't try to manage the situation on your own. Inform her parents of your concerns.

Overinvolved Parents

Chapter 2 talked about communicating effectively with parents. Let's take a brief look now at some of the issues that parental involvement in youth sport presents.

Family relationships can be strongly affected by youth sports participation. Most of us have witnessed the extreme behavior of what has become generically known as the "Little League parent." Most parents would never dream of acting in such a manner, but even while offering support, some parents become so emotionally involved with their daughter's participation in youth sports that what they see as encouragement comes to be seen by the child as pressure. The line is crossed when the young athlete begins to think that her parents' attention is *dependent* on her participation (or, even, performing well). What a dilemma for the child! If she quits, she believes she will lose her parents' support and attention, in other words, love. If she continues playing but fails to excel, she will expect negative feedback from her parents. Finally, if she does excel, the bar will be raised along with expectations, increasing the pressure.

Saying all that, most families are able to make the youth sports experience a fulfilling one. If parent-child interaction is independent of athletic performance and the child is encouraged to have fun and try her best, the experience will likely be a positive one for all involved.

Sexual Harassment

Coaches are authority figures. They control roster spots, practice regimens, and playing time. They generally have complete control over their athletes (and staff). This is true with any age group, but particularly so when coaching youngsters because you have the dual dynamic of coach/player and adult/child at work. In today's hypersensitive climate, it is important that you display appropriate behavior with your athletes at all times. While physical contact (a pat on the shoulder, a ruffling of the hair) can be an important aspect of affirming a young player's value, not all players will be comfortable with all behaviors. You should take great pains to avoid any behavior that might be misconstrued by one of your players or coaches.

Think of sexual harassment as being perceptual in nature. If the receiver feels uncomfortable, then the onus is on the perpetrator to change his or her behavior. Sexual harassment can be explicit (overtly stated) or implicit (not clearly stated, but understood). An example might be a promise, or withholding, of playing time tied to a player's submission to sexual advances. While many factors go into determining what constitutes sexual harassment, the pressing issue is whether the relationship between the two people is of an unequal nature, thereby giving one party a coercive position.

When all is said and done, there are far more similarities between young boys and girls than there are differences. Young children all need support and understanding. They are eager to learn and are enthusiastic in their pursuits. What a wonderful opportunity for you, their coach and teacher, to instill the values and habits that will help shape who they are and to break down the kinds of gender stereotyping that limit who they will become. At the same time, be sensitive to the ways in which boys and girls differ. Doing so will allow you to hone your coaching approach for maximum effectiveness. Show you care, create a positive environment for learning, and be consistent in your approach. You will make a difference in their young lives that will be looked back upon and valued more greatly with each passing year.

4

BASKETBALL BASICS

NOW THAT YOU have a general understanding of the qualities and interpersonal skills required to be a successful coach, it's time to look at some basketball basics. Let's take a look at equipment needs, player positions, staffing needs, and the rules of basketball.

EQUIPMENT

One of the greatest attractions of basketball is that it requires so little equipment. All a player really needs are a pair of shoes, a basketball, and a basket. Because of this, basketball is among the most accessible of sports, cutting across socioeconomic boundaries and geographical barriers. Of course, as a coach desiring to teach the game, you will want to give careful consideration to playing equipment, teaching aids, and apparel. Let's take a look at a few.

Playing Equipment

Basketball

The size and weight of the ball should be proportionate to the size and age level of the participants. The standard women's basketball is 28.5 inches in circumference and weighs between 18 and 20 ounces.

This will likely be suitable for most older players, but perhaps unwieldy for many younger athletes, due to their small hands, stature, and lack of strength. Fortunately, smaller balls are being manufactured today that are designed specifically for youth leagues and are a fine alternative for younger players.

Shoes

A boundless selection awaits those looking for basketball shoes. Each of the top athletic shoe manufacturers markets dozens of models in a dizzying array of styles and colors, all in an effort to set the "trend." And, naturally, most kids chase those trends, embracing style and aesthetics over substance.

But what should a parent look for in a shoe? Comfort and good traction are a must. Don't be concerned with ankle support. Today's 3/4-tops and low-tops don't offer much support anyway. That's what taping or ankle braces (see following) are for. Also, most kids favor the lightest shoes, but sometimes extremely light shoes fail to provide the cushioning or support necessary to offset all the pounding the legs and feet take in the course of play. This is not as much of a problem for younger players, however, because their lighter body weight does not generate the same force on their legs. The good news is that there are plenty of quality low-to-moderately priced shoes on the market, many of them produced by the "big name" shoe companies. The bad news is that trend-chasing kids may not want to be caught dead wearing them.

Coaching Tip

Encourage players to carry their basketball shoes to the gym and to change shoes when they arrive rather than wearing them from home. This prolongs the life of the shoes, limiting their wear and tear to the smooth gym floor. Also, this keeps the dust and grime from outdoors from being brought onto the court.

Keep in mind that basketball shoes are not necessary to play the game. Cross-trainers can be adequate, as can other types of all-court shoes. Running shoes should be avoided, however, as they lack the stability for lateral movement.

Ankle Braces

By far the most common injury in basketball is the ankle sprain. Play the game long enough, and it will happen to you. Ankle braces not only offer the support that today's shoes do not, but many of them offer support comparable to a good ankle taping. Ankle braces won't necessarily prevent ankle sprains, but they will significantly reduce the severity of an injury. Some players may complain that braces feel bulky or are uncomfortable. Some players just don't like the look of ankle braces. The older the player, the more important this equipment is.

Socks

Generally, two pairs of athletic socks are recommended, both for comfort and for preventing blisters.

Apparel

Athletic shorts and a loose-fitting, breathable shirt are best. If resources allow, reversible, two-color tank-top jerseys make practice organization more flexible. Have your school or team's name printed on these jerseys so that your players have a practice uniform. You may also wish to get a half-dozen or so "pennies" (mesh pullover jerseys) in a third color for use in drills that require dividing the team into more than two groups.

Safety Equipment

Mouth guards protect teeth from sharp elbows, but many players don't like to wear them because of discomfort or because they impede talking clearly. Safety glasses or goggles offer eye protection for those seeking such, while elbow and kneepads provide additional protection to limbs.

Teaching Aids

Thumb through any athletic equipment supply catalog and you'll see a million items and devices designed to teach the game of basketball: dribbling goggles, shooting-form devices, jump ropes. Some are superfluous, but effective. Some are junk. All are a luxury. Of course, if you have an unlimited budget then, by all means, shop to your heart's content. But, really, there are only a few items that are essential to conducting practices and playing games.

The most obvious item is a whistle. It is a universal signal that tells players and coaches alike that you want their attention. I know some coaches (myself among them) who don't like whistles and use them sparingly. But, believe me, you'll have situations that call for one, especially, say, when coaching a team of chatty 8- or 9-year-olds the day after the release of the new CD from the Backstreet Boys!

Another must-have is a clipboard (yes, there's a reason all TV and movie portrayals of coaches include clipboards!) of some sort. You'll need to keep track of practice plans, rosters, offensive and defensive diagrams, emergency phone numbers, and the like. The better mousetrap to handle this need has yet to be invented.

Plastic cones or low-profile discs are other inexpensive teaching tools. They can be placed at any point on the court as reference points for drills, teaching sessions, and conditioning workouts. They are lightweight, take up very little storage space, and, most important, do not present a physical hazard to players.

PLAYERS AND POSITIONS

Basketball is not a game of specialization. Football may have its offensive and defensive squads, while baseball has pitchers, position players, and even the designated hitter. But in basketball, you must possess a wide array of skills to be effective. Every player should be able to:

- Pivot
- Pass and catch the basketball
- Dribble with either hand
- Defend opponents on the perimeter or in the post area
- Block out and rebound
- Shoot the basketball

Don't expect players to have equal ability in all these areas. One of your most important responsibilities when coaching young players is to help them develop all of their individual skills to the greatest extent possible, building on their strengths and shoring up their weaknesses (we will discuss this in greater detail in chapter 7).

Throughout this book, symbols are used within the figures for different movements, player and staff designations, and so forth. Figure 4.1 provides a guide to these symbols.

Player Positions

Naturally, every young player brings with her a different array of physical attributes and basketball skills. Some players are tall, some are short. Some are fast, while others lack great footspeed. Some will relish contact and the physical aspects of the game, while others are more finesse-oriented. Within any team, you will find a broad range of shooting, dribbling, and passing skills. Each player's attributes lend themselves to a certain position (or positions). See figure 4.2 for a layout of player positions.

The following is a brief, general discussion of five primary offensive positions in basketball and the characteristics most desired in each. For ease of diagramming plays, coaches may either use numbers or abbreviations to show which player goes where. In this book, numbers are used.

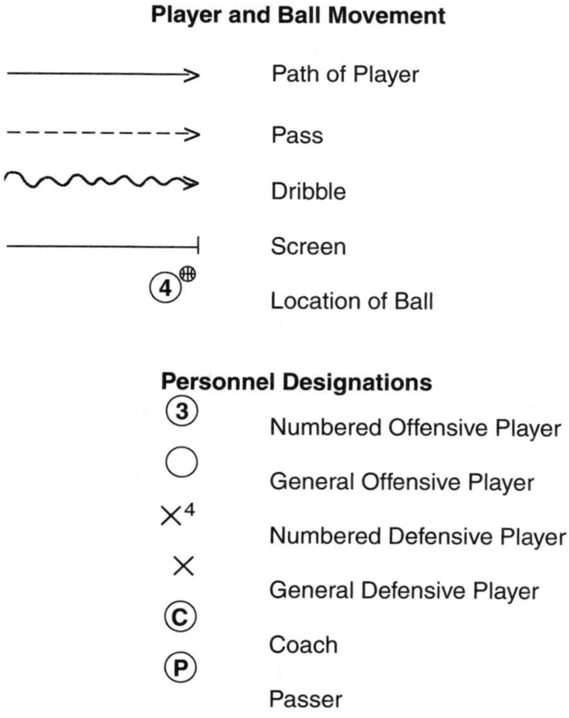

1. Point guard (PG, or 1). Likely to be your best passer and dribbler, the point guard is the player that most systems designate to run the offense. In more sophisticated systems and in high school play and

Player and Ball Movement

⟶	Path of Player
- - - -⟶	Pass
∿∿∿⟶	Dribble
⟶⊢	Screen
④⊕	Location of Ball

Personnel Designations

③	Numbered Offensive Player
◯	General Offensive Player
✕⁴	Numbered Defensive Player
✕	General Defensive Player
Ⓒ	Coach
Ⓟ	Passer

FIGURE 4.1
Symbols key

beyond, this player is often your "coach on the floor" and should have a clear understanding of what the team is trying to do. Often shorter and quicker than many of the other players, the point guard should have the ability to penetrate defenses off the dribble and to read the defense so as to make good choices regarding whom to pass the ball to. She does not have to be a great shooter or scorer (though it's nice if she is), but she should be capable enough to keep opposing defenses honest. But the most important attribute of a point guard is "court sense," that innate understanding of the game that allows for good decision making in a fast-paced environment. This last characteristic makes the point guard the rarest treasure in the game, since few players possess it in abundance. This is particularly true in youth basketball, where players are just learning and haven't played enough competitively to develop a sense for the game. Still, it will be obvious that some of your players have a natural understanding of the game. One of them will become your next point guard.

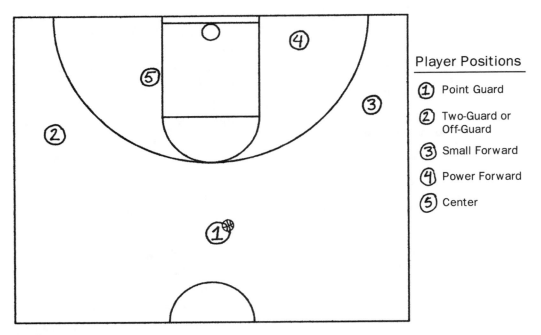

FIGURE 4.2
Half-court showing player positions

2. Shooting guard (2G, or 2). Sometimes called the "two-guard" or "off-guard," the shooting guard is usually one of the best outside shooters on your team. She should also be able to handle the ball well so as to share some of the play-making responsibilities with the point guard. She should be a good passer so as to take advantage of opportunities to get the ball inside to your post players (power forward and center).

3. Small forward (SF, or 3). The small forward is a bit of a hybrid position, often bigger than your guards (though perhaps not quite as quick or as proficient a dribbler) but smaller than your post players (though you'll need her to rebound and play effectively near the basket). She should possess many of the same outside shooting and passing skills as the guards. She should also be like a post player, able to defend players close to the basket and to rebound effectively, especially at the offensive end of the floor.

4. Power forward (PF, or 4). Your power forward should be one of your biggest and strongest players, able to rebound at both ends of the floor. She will be able to post up (get good offensive position near the basket) opposing defenders in order to get inside shots. But she should also be able to play facing the basket and to make the short perimeter shot. Most important, the power forward should enjoy the physical aspects of playing near the basket: defense, rebounding, and offensive positioning in the low post, all of which involve physical contact.

5. Center (C, or 5). Sometimes called the "post," the center position is often filled by your tallest player, making it easier for her to maneuver close to the basket. Unlike your guards and forwards, the center usually plays with her back to the basket in the low post on offense and should be an inside scoring threat. She does not have to be a particularly good dribbler, but should have "soft hands" that enable her to catch a variety of passes in traffic. She will also be your "last line" of defense, protecting the basket and making it difficult for your opponent to get good shots around the hoop.

Perimeter and Post

Although I have just provided a brief description of each player position, when it comes to youth basketball in particular, every effort should be made to avoid pigeonholing players into a single, specific position. Designating positions by name or number may be necessary for alignment and teaching purposes, but don't use them to limit your players. (In later chapters, you will find diagrams that use numerical designations to make the sequences easier to follow.)

In general, you should endeavor to think of your playing positions as being divided into two general groups: perimeter and posts. *Perimeter* players have the ability to play facing the basket. *Post* players have the skills necessary to play inside with their backs to the basket.

You will find that some players have the skills to do both. Versatility is a good thing and should be encouraged. To designate a young girl as a small forward or a center without giving her the chance to try other positions or to develop other skills is a disservice to her. Obviously, having every player play every position on the floor is impractical because the players will get confused. But certainly, young players should be given the opportunity to play more than one position during the season.

POST PLAYER DEVELOPMENT

Be aware that many taller young girls may be self-conscious of their height. Girls mature faster than boys and reach their full height at a younger age. Because of this, coordination for taller girls takes longer to develop than it does for their shorter counterparts. So your post players may be somewhat gangly and awkward compared with your other players, and they may lack the strength to compete effectively in physical situations. Posts tend to develop at a slower pace than perimeter players, so be patient.

Many young post players become frustrated because the game does not come easy to them, as it seems to for their teammates. Many are hesitant to try to develop new skills because they feel awkward and self-conscious when trying them. Be enthusiastic with your posts, complimenting them for even the most incremental improvements in skill development. I use terms like "smooth," "balanced," and "graceful" a lot to give them a sense that they are moving well and look good in their execution. I try to use adjectives that have positive connotations when describing the particulars of a specific skill. For example, I may say to a young girl, when discussing establishing a low-post position, "Use those long legs of yours to seal off the defender and make yourself available for the pass." Said in passing, and without undue emphasis, these kinds of comments can have a very positive effect over time, allowing young post players to view their size as the positive attribute it is as opposed to the curse they may perceive it to be.

If your system is such that your perimeter (1, 2, and 3) and post positions (4 and 5) have essentially the same responsibilities within their group, you'll have a flexible situation in which players can play more than one spot on the floor. (*Note:* This is true even if you have your point guard running the show. Your offense should be designed in a manner that any of your perimeter players can start your offense.) In other words, your players should be interchangeable within the subgroups of perimeter and posts, and a few players, particularly those who might be traditionally viewed as small or power forwards, may be able to play both in the post and on the perimeter.

There is a practical side to viewing players as perimeter and posts. It gives you greater flexibility in terms of player combinations on the floor. For example, it's not necessary to have a point guard, shooting guard, and small forward on the floor at a given time. You could choose to play three shooting guards together or two point guards and a small forward. This allows different players to play alongside each other. It also makes it easier for you to adjust when players may be absent due to vacations, family social events, dentist appointments, and the like. You don't want to be in a situation where both of your centers are gone for two weeks on vacation and your "system" comes to a standstill. It'll make you wish you were in Barbados yourself.

Coaching Tip

Designating player positions based on height is not always a good idea. Be open-minded. Young girls develop at wildly different rates, and it may well be that one of your tallest players is more of a point guard than a post. Let your players play to their strengths. Avoid stereotyping them because of their appearance.

STAFFING

As mentioned in earlier chapters, coaching youth basketball involves a tremendous amount of teaching. The necessity of giving individual attention to players and conducting drill work in small groups means that you will need assistant coaches to help you manage the team. At the youth level, your assistants will be volunteers, often parents who wish to help out with their daughter's activities. Sometimes you may find a local high school or college student who is interested in coaching and would love to get her feet wet by helping out. While you will no doubt welcome the help of anyone dedicated enough to put in the time and energy to work with young children, there are some things to consider before taking someone on board:

- **Background check.** Unfortunately, in today's society, this is a must. Unless you know the prospective assistant very well, a background check should be conducted on any individual before allowing him or her to work with young people. This will reduce the chance that anyone with a prior history of problems involving children will have access to such an environment again.

- **Philosophy.** Does this person share your perspective on youth sports and agree with what you are trying to accomplish with the team? This is important not so much in terms of basketball philosophy (offense, defense), but life philosophy (the values and lessons you wish to teach). You want to be on the same page.

- **Commitment.** Even though it is likely a volunteer position, the assistant coaches should be willing to attend all practices and games. The players will benefit from the continuity and familiarity, and you'll appreciate the flexibility it gives you in planning practices.

Coaching Tip

If a parent offers assistance, try to gain a sense of whether the daughter wants to be coached by her parent. If so, and if you feel that the parent's perspective is healthy and balanced, accept the offer. If you have doubts about the player/parent dynamic, or if you believe the parent's presence might create tension or conflict, then gracefully decline.

Assistant coaches serve many functions. At practice, under your leadership, they help conduct and supervise drills and player development. They must be good teachers and exhibit tremendous patience. They should bring a positive attitude to practices and games and an enthusiasm that makes the game fun for the players. Your assistants should be in basic agreement with what you're trying to accomplish but should be able to offer different perspectives at times (you want loyalty, but not "yes" people, surrounding you).

ATTENDANT PERSONNEL

Once you have an assistant coach on board, it's time to look at other responsibilities that need coverage. Whether it be medical supervision, transportation, or statistical coverage, you need to be sure that you have reliable, competent people in place.

Certified athletic trainers are professionals who have extensive backgrounds in the prevention and treatment of athletic injuries. Many youth leagues have game covered by an athletic trainer or, occasionally, a local volunteer physician. The trainers should have access to ice and a training kit stocked with bandages, surgical gloves, athletic tape, and other items necessary for the treatment of minor injuries. They should also have access to a set of crutches. A cell phone is a must since, these days, public phones on school grounds are often unavailable and unreliable.

You may also want to enlist many of your players' parents for transportation duty. This is particularly important if your league involves any sort of travel or if you will be taking your team to area tournaments. Spell out this expectation at your pre-season parents' orientation meeting described in chapter 2. Let them know that everyone's cooperation would be greatly appreciated.

Depending on the competitive level at which you are coaching, you may wish to ask some of your parents to videotape games or to keep statistics. Involving your players' parents not only helps you, it also gives parents a sense of participation. And, who knows, they might be so focused on carrying out the task assigned to them that they will forget to yell at the referees! Of course, the flip side is that they may feel like a more integral part of the team and, therefore, may feel less hesitation at offering coaching "advice."

THE RULES OF THE GAME

Basketball is a game of movement, where ten players are in near-constant motion, cutting, screening, running, and jumping. Some physical contact is inevitable, especially in youth basketball. Players' coordination is still developing, and the frequent confusion over where they are supposed to go (I'm sorry to say that no matter how great a coaching job you do, your offense will sometimes look like an unorganized fire drill) results in lots of abrupt directional changes, bumps, and pushes.

Let's look at some aspects of the rules of basketball.

The Size of the Court

Basketball courts come in many different lengths and widths. Even though the standard high school court is 84 feet long, many courts are shorter, depending on the space available at the time of construction. Many youth league games are played on side-courts, which are used mostly for practice purposes by older teams. These courts can be significantly shorter, allowing younger players to compete without getting too tired. Fortunately, court markings are pretty much consistent, so there is a uniformity to the game that makes it easier to teach and play. Review figure 4.3 and familiarize yourself with the basket-

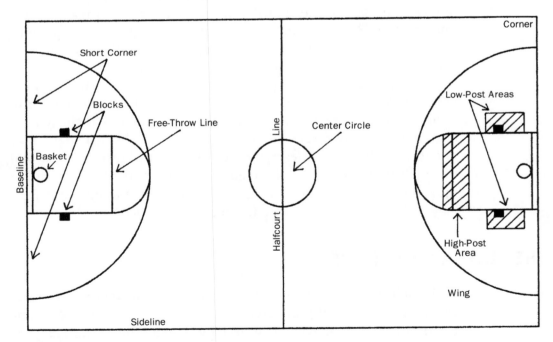

FIGURE 4.3
Layout of a basketball court

ball court and the names of the markings. We will discuss court terminology in greater depth at the beginning of chapter 7.

The Height of the Basket

Regulation basket height is 10 feet, but that is beyond the capabilities of many younger players. As a result, they will revert to throwing the ball at the basket in an effort to reach the hoop. This reinforces poor shooting mechanics and heightens the sense of frustration that failure can bring. It is important to scale down not only the physical size of the court but the basket height as well. This can be accomplished either by the use of adjustable portable baskets or, in the face of older fixed-height baskets, the purchase of backboard or basket devices that slip over the existing hoop and create a new backboard and basket of a more accommodating height. While there is no strict standard by age group, a good rule of thumb is 8 feet for ages 7–8, 9 feet for ages 9–11, and 10 feet for ages 12–13. Naturally you'll have some 8-year-olds who can comfortably reach a 10-foot basket while some 11-year-olds might struggle with the 9-foot height. Still, in general, these adjustments should make for a more enjoyable and successful experience for all involved.

The Role of Officials

Officiating a youth basketball game is an exercise in pursuing a balance between strict adherence to the rules of the game and allowing the players to actually play. At the youngest ages, players will often travel or double dribble in an effort to advance the basketball. If officials called every transgression, the game would never be played. While they don't want to ignore obvious infringements, youth league referees should try to officiate with an eye toward advantage/disadvantage. In other words, if a player travels with the ball but does not gain an appreciable advantage on her opponent, then there is no call. There needs to be some semblance of flow and rhythm to a game, and blowing the whistle every 15 seconds is going to be unsettling. As the players get older and their coordination and skills improve, the standard becomes higher. By the time they reach high school,

Coaching Tip

Most officials are truly working hard to call the best game possible. They are not playing favorites or making calls deliberately for or against a specific team. Youth league officials are usually young, often high school students. They may be inexperienced and can easily miss a call or two, but they're not out to get you and there's nothing personal involved. Treat them with respect and consideration.

players should be held strictly accountable on fouls and violations.

Officials are also responsible for ensuring good sportsmanship on behalf of the players and coaches. In turn, the officials are working hard to make the game safe and fair for everyone involved, and they should be treated with respect and courtesy. Do not allow your players to argue with the referees or exhibit unsportsmanlike behavior. In turn, you should be a role model for your players by the manner with which you conduct yourself.

The Length of the Game

Games are played in either two halves or four quarters. The length of the game should depend on the age group involved. The younger the age, the shorter the game (although, if you have many players on your team, you might prefer longer games to give everyone playing time). In general, the game clock stops on fouls, violations, when the ball goes out of bounds, and for time-outs. Many leagues now use a "running" clock that does not stop except for time-outs. This method makes game lengths more uniform, allowing leagues to better stay on schedule. It also reduces the need for a person to sit at the game-table to operate the clock.

Fouls

Illegal contact comes in many forms, but usually officials call fouls based on these general considerations:

- A player (offensive or defensive) who establishes a position on the floor has rights to that spot and cannot be displaced through physical force.
- Whichever player initiates the contact is the likely offender.
- A player cannot use her hands, arms, or legs to stop a player from moving. Rather, she must move her body between the

other player and where she is going, forcing the other player to change direction.

As mentioned earlier, contact is inevitable in basketball. The key is whether it results in an advantage for one player or another. Here are the most prevalent kinds of common, non-shooting fouls:

- **Blocking.** Bumping and physically impeding a moving player
- **Holding.** Grabbing or restricting a player's movement by using the hands or arms (hand-checking falls into this category)
- **Illegal screen.** Also called a moving screen, the screener is not completely set, or stopped, when contact with the screened defender is made
- **Over the back.** A rebounding foul that occurs when a player makes contact with a player who has proper position and is attempting to rebound
- **Charging.** An offensive foul where an offensive player runs into or displaces a defensive player who has established position

A shooting foul occurs when an offensive player is fouled while attempting a shot at the basket. Two free throws are awarded.

Officials may also call technical or flagrant fouls. The former has to do with player or coaching conduct. The latter is called when a foul that uses unnecessary force or that puts a player's safety at risk is committed. By being a good role model for your players and by stressing the importance of respect and sportsmanship, you will avoid having to deal with these types of fouls.

A team that fouls too much will suffer the consequences. Too many team fouls in a quarter or half will put the opposing team in a bonus situation, where players will be awarded free throws for even common fouls. In addition, a player who commits five personal fouls is disqualified and must leave the game.

Violations

Violations (as opposed to fouls) usually involve ballhandling or time miscues. These turnovers, or loss of possession of the ball, are frequent occurrences in youth basketball. The most common violations are:

- **Traveling.** By far the most frequent transgression, this occurs when a player takes more than one step without dribbling the ball. This can occur at the start or finish of a dribbling episode. Palming, or carrying, the ball is also a form of traveling.
- **Double dribble.** This is another frequent violation. It involves dribbling the ball with both hands at the same time *or* recommencing a dribble after having stopped dribbling the first time.
- **Three seconds in the lane.** If a player stands in the lane at their offensive end of the floor for more than 3 consecutive seconds, it is a violation. Most officials will warn players that they are camping in the lane and will only blow the whistle if the players fail to adjust.
- **Five-second rule.** An offensive player holds the ball for more than 5 seconds, without passing or dribbling, while being closely defended. A 5-second rule also applies to an offensive player inbounding (starting play by throwing the ball in from out-of-bounds) the ball, as they need to do so in that short time span.

Other types of violations include over-and-back (retreating into the backcourt with the ball after having crossed the midcourt line), entering the lane too early on a free throw attempt, or crossing the baseline or sideline when inbounding the ball.

With your equipment needs met, staffing in place, and grasp of the rules fortified, you are now ready to teach the game to your players. But before your players can begin learning, they need to be prepared physically for the demands basketball places on the body. Chapter 5 deals with helping your players prepare physically for the challenges ahead.

5

CONDITIONING
FOR BASKETBALL

MOST PARENTS WOULD laugh at the necessity of physically conditioning young athletes so that they could play basketball. After all, just wind children up and they *go all day!* Still, even with the natural energy levels that most children possess, it is a good idea to give some attention to proper conditioning, for the sake of both performance and safety. Muscles unaccustomed to strenuous physical activity need to be prepared for the exertion of playing basketball. A 2001 study by the Centers for Disease Control and Prevention showed that, among children and young adults, nearly one-quarter of all emergency room visits during 1997 and 1998 were the result of sports-related injuries. Of those, basketball led the way, accounting for 17.1 percent of all sports injuries. While some of these injuries (for example, sprained ankles) are an inherent risk of participation, many others can be prevented or minimized through proper physical conditioning.

Conditioning for any physical activity consists of three components: *flexibility and agility, strength,* and *endurance.* This chapter discusses all three areas and how they relate to the young athlete.

FLEXIBILITY AND AGILITY

Flexibility developed through stretching is one of the most undervalued components of balanced physical conditioning. Too often, proper stretching is ignored because of time constraints or a general lack of appreciation of its importance in maintaining a fit body. Even though children's bodies tend to be naturally limber, muscle tightness can occur when they're beginning a new physical activity. For the youngest children, stretching may not be absolutely necessary (as it will be in later years), but I believe it's a good idea to develop the habit early, establishing a routine they'll come to think of as second nature in years to come.

Warm Up Dynamically

Stretching should be preceded by a brief warm-up designed to elevate the heart rate slightly and to warm the muscles. *Do not stretch cold muscles.* I believe strongly in utilizing a dynamic warm-up. In other words, prepare the players for stretching with a variety of physical movements, not simply skipping rope or running around the gym a couple of times. The dynamic warm-up also helps develop agility, balance, and footwork, crucial elements in the sport of basketball.

To conduct a dynamic warm-up, have players line up in groups of three or four. Each of the following segments should be conducted in a controlled, relaxed manner. Remember, the idea is to loosen the body and prepare for the stretching regimen. This phase is not meant to overly exert the players. Here is a sample of a dynamic warm-up executed on the basketball court:

Coaching Tip

Practice time in the gym is a precious commodity. You may have only an hour of floor time, so make the most of it. Consider warming up and stretching prior to taking the floor. Conduct your warm-ups outside, weather permitting. Or use a hallway or corridor.

- **Easy jog.** Begin with an easy jog to the far end of the court. Encourage your players to start slowly. Have them dangle and shake their arms as they jog, helping to loosen the upper body. Once everyone has reached the far end, have the players return the same way. Do this twice, increasing the pace to about half-speed the second time through.

- **Heel walk.** Have players walk to midcourt on their heels, toes pointed up as far as possible. After reaching midcourt, they walk normally to the far end. They return by walking toe-up to midcourt and normally from midcourt back to the end.

- **Skipping.** Have players skip the length of the court and back, using a short, quick motion. The key here is that they should keep their toes *up* the entire time (most children point the toes of their airborne foot down when skipping). Encourage them to use their arms in a pumping action to help their vertical momentum.

- **Carioca.** Some know this as a "grapevine." This right-foot-over-left, left-foot-over-right lateral motion emphasizes rotating the hips (which should rotate 90 degrees with each twist) and upper body and is an excellent full-body warm-up. Tell players to extend their arms out from the side to help maintain balance. Have them do this twice, up and back across the width of the court.

- **Backward jog.** This is not backward *running!* It is a jog, and the emphasis should be on reaching up and back as high as possible with the heel. Done properly, the players will not make rapid progress down the floor. Rather, they will feel almost as if they're leaning forward even as they're jogging backward. Up and back one time.

- **Forward run/Backward run.** At about three-quarter speed, have your players run to midcourt, turn on the run, and finish with a backward run. Have them return in the same manner. Repeat.

Feel free to add your own elements to a dynamic warm-up, keeping the routine fresh for your players. Just remember to emphasize slower, controlled movements. It's not a competition or a race!

Stretching

After warming up, take the time to stretch out the following major muscle groups: quadriceps (thighs), hamstrings, calves, groin, lower back, upper back, and shoulders. There are a variety of stretches for each muscle group, but most athletes eventually settle on a series

KEYS TO STRETCHING

1. Warm up *before* stretching; don't ever stretch cold muscles.

2. Stretch daily, even when not working out.

3. Stretch large muscle groups first, then move on to smaller muscles.

4. Make your movements gradual and relaxed. Avoid bouncing.

5. Stretching should not be painful. Sore is okay, but any discomfort should be mild and should not last long.

6. Don't hold your breath. Breathe naturally throughout the stretching routine.

7. Perform each stretch two to three times.

8. Stretch *after* workouts as well. This will reduce tightness and soreness.

that works for them. However, it is likely that your young athletes will need guidance and supervision as they go through their stretching routine. Stretching can also be seen as a social time for your athletes, a chance to talk with each other and bond. This can be important for team chemistry. Just make sure they're actually stretching while they talk.

When stretching, emphasize a slow, steady stretch. Tell your players to try not to bounce when stretching. Instead, the motion should be gradual and relaxed, taking the muscle just past the comfort point. Players should feel some tension on the muscle and possibly some mild soreness. If they feel a sharp pain, they should stop. The following descriptions are written to you. Simply pass this information on to your athletes!

Coaching Tip

Try "CRAC-king" joints and muscles. *Contract, relax, and contract.* Stretch the muscle for 10–15 seconds. Relax for 5–7 seconds. Restretch for 10–15 seconds again. You'll be able to stretch further with each repetition.

Quadriceps Stretch

To stretch the top of the thigh, lie on your left side. Grasp the right ankle or foot and gently pull the right leg back. Be sure to keep your knees and hips aligned. Do not arch your back. (See figure 5.1.) Turn to your right side and repeat with the left leg.

FIGURE 5.1
Quadriceps stretch

Hamstring Stretch

To stretch the back of the upper leg, lie on your back with both knees bent and your feet on the floor. Grab the left leg just behind the knee, and, with the left leg extended, gently pull it back toward your chest. The left knee can be slightly bent; the left foot should be flexed. (See figure 5.2.) Repeat with the right leg.

FIGURE 5.2
Hamstring stretch

Upper Calf Stretch

To stretch the upper calf, lean against a wall with arms extended in front of you. Step forward with the left foot, knee bent. Keep the right knee locked and the right heel on the floor. The further forward you lean, the more you'll feel the stretch in your right leg. (See figure 5.3.) Repeat with the other leg.

FIGURE 5.3
Upper calf stretch

FIGURE 5.4
Lower calf/Achilles stretch

Lower Calf/Achilles Stretch

To stretch the Achilles' tendon, perform a similar stretch as for the upper calf stretch. However, bend the right knee slightly. Still keep your right heel on the floor. (See figure 5.4.) Repeat with the other leg.

Lower Back Stretch

To stretch the lower back, keep both feet even and lean against wall with forearms. Tilt your pelvis toward the wall. Initially, stand close to the wall, with your feet approximately 12 to 18 inches from the base. (See figure 5.5.) For a bigger stretch, move your feet further back from the wall.

Butterfly Stretch

To stretch the groin and inner thighs, sit on the floor and put the soles of your feet together. Hold your ankles and lean forward, keeping your back straight. Press your elbows against your knees, pushing them toward the floor. (See figure 5.6.) For a bigger stretch, bring your heels closer to your body.

FIGURE 5.5
Lower back stretch

FIGURE 5.6
Butterfly stretch

Trunk Twist

To stretch the lower back and hip, sit on the floor with the right foot over the extended left leg. The right foot should rest just even with the outside of your left knee. Rotating your trunk to the right, place your left elbow against the outside of your right knee and push back against it, all the time rotating your torso to the right. (See figure 5.7.) Switch legs and repeat.

FIGURE 5.7
Trunk twist

Chest/Shoulder Stretch

To stretch the chest and the front of the shoulders, clasp your hands behind your back, palms facing away from body. Rotate your shoulders back, and raise your hands back and away from the body. Don't bend over at the waist. (See figure 5.8.)

Triceps/Shoulder Stretch

To stretch the shoulders and the back of the arm, reach up and over with your left hand in an attempt to touch the middle of your back. Your left elbow should be pointed skyward. Use your right hand to pull the left elbow back, increasing the stretch. (See figure 5.9.) Repeat with your right arm.

Upper Back/Shoulder Stretch

To stretch the upper back and back of shoulders, bring your left arm across your chest and use your right hand to pull the left arm from above the elbow to a full stretch. Don't rotate your torso. (See figure 5.10.) Repeat with the right arm.

FIGURE 5.8
Chest/Shoulder stretch

FIGURE 5.9
Triceps/Shoulder stretch

FIGURE 5.10
Upper back/Shoulder stretch

TRIED, BUT NOT TRUE

Some types of stretches are not only ineffective, they can also be harmful. Avoid these Big Three at all costs!

- **Hurdler's stretch.** Sitting with one leg extended and the other bent back to your side, you reach out to touch your toes. This puts far too much stress on your knees and hips.

- **Toe touches.** Standing, with knees locked out, you bend over and touch your toes. This does a poor job of stretching the hamstrings because they aren't isolated adequately. Moreover, it places stress on the lower back.

- **Full sit-ups.** While not technically a stretch, it is among the most common of exercises. It's also criminal for the lower back. Think "crunches" (later in this chapter) and *only* crunches.

STRENGTH TRAINING

Strength training does not necessarily mean *weight* training. While weights may be an important part of a strength training regimen for older athletes, children's developing bodies do not necessarily need, nor are they prepared for, high-intensity strength training. At the youngest ages, any involvement in sports should emphasize skill acquisition and development. Strength development can be gradually phased in as the young athlete matures. Expert opinions vary, but as a general rule, I would not encourage weight training until the athlete enters high school.

Up until high school age, a young athlete can improve her strength by using resistance exercises that utilize body weight, such as push-ups, dips, sit-ups, lunges, and pull-ups. For many young girls, completing even a single

Coaching Tip

It is almost more important to stretch *after* practice than before. However, very few coaches take the time to do so. Plan for 5–10 minutes at the end of practice to re-stretch, to help your players avoid tight muscles and soreness.

pull-up or push-up can be a challenge. Those whose strength is still developing can enjoy the advantages these exercises afford by doing "negatives." A negative rep simply means doing only the "easier" part of the exercise. For example, a negative pull-up would be to start in the chin-over-the-bar position and slowly lower yourself to full extension. Then have someone lift you back to the starting point, and again lower yourself. Do this until you reach muscle failure (cannot lower yourself slowly). Gradually, over time, your strength will improve and you will be able to complete the entire exercise on your own. The same approach can be used for push-ups, dips, and lunges.

For those coaches and athletes who insist on beginning strength training with weights prior to high school, let me give one strong piece of advice: *Keep it simple!* There are many, many different strength-training programs out there, and most of them are beneficial in some manner. But strength-training regimens are like diets: A new fad comes along almost daily. Rather than attempting to process every new theory that comes down the fitness highway, stick to the simple premise of *push/pull/legs*. For every *push* (bench press, incline press, triceps extension, push-up, dip) exercise you do, also do a *pull* (lat pull, seated row, upright row, biceps curl, pull-up). Complement those upper-body lifts with at least two leg exercises (quads and hamstrings). A workout consisting of three pulls, three pushes, and two legs (three sets of each exercise) is a more than adequate in-season routine. In the off season, an expanded routine might be preferable. Just be sure to maintain the same ratio of push-to-pull exercises.

Perhaps the most important element in any strength-training program is abdominal work. The "abs" and lower back are dependent on each other. Weak abs will often lead to lower-back problems. I would suggest incorporating an ab and back routine into your team's stretching regimen. It does not have to be elaborate. Of the following two abdominal exercises and two back strengtheners, try to incorporate one each into your stretching each day.

Coaching Tip

Adjust your strength-training program every couple of months to keep athletes from getting stale. Substituting new lifts or changing the number of sets and repetitions will keep your athletes motivated and working hard.

FORM *IS* FUNCTION!

The key to any abdominal and back routine is proper form while performing the exercise. Avoid these common mistakes:

- It is *not* a hip flexor, neck, and shoulder routine. Keep these areas quiet!
- Don't pull your neck when performing movement. Keep your chin from rotating toward your chest. In fact, try pushing your head *backward*, thus reducing pressure on the neck.
- Don't use momentum; lunging through an exercise allows your muscles to relax. Focus on a smooth, constant motion throughout.
- Don't arch your back on abdominal work. Think "Tailbone to the floor" at all times.

Crunches

Crunches work your abs. To start, lie prone, with knees bent. Hands can either be behind your head or crossed in front over your chest. Raise your ribs to clear the shoulder blades *just* off the floor. (See figure 5.11.) Rotate your shoulders slightly toward your knees. *Do not pull your head up and forward with your hands.* Focus on pressing the tailbone to the floor. Hold, then slowly lower to the starting position. Continue crunching to muscle exhaustion.

FIGURE 5.11
Abdominal crunches

Twisting Crunch

Similar to the basic crunch, twisting crunches also work the abs. Press your right shoulder to the floor and rotate the left shoulder (*not* your elbow!) up and toward the right knee. (See figure 5.12.) Return to starting position. Alternate sides with each repetition.

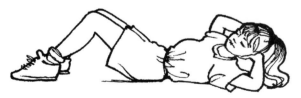

FIGURE 5.12
Twisting crunch

Arm and Leg Extension

Arm and leg extensions work the upper and lower back. Start on all fours. Keep your head straight and your feet flexed. Lift your right leg straight out behind you until it is parallel to the floor. Simultaneously, lift your left arm until it, too, is parallel to the floor. (See figure 5.13.) Hold for 5–10 seconds. Repeat with the opposite side. Start with five reps on each side. Be sure to keep abs firmly contracted and don't arch your back.

FIGURE 5.13
Arm and leg extension

Dead Bugs

If nothing else, your kids will have a blast with the name! This exercise works the lower back. Lie on your back with arms perpendicular to the floor. Raise your feet off the floor so that your knees are bent to 90 degrees and your calves are parallel to the floor. Lift shoulders slightly off the floor, pressing tailbone down. Now the fun starts! Simultaneously lower your right arm back behind you while straightening your left leg toward the floor (without foot touching). (See figure 5.14.) The key is to keep your *left* arm and *right* leg completely still while doing this. Think it's easy? Try it! Return to starting position and then repeat with the opposite side. This exercise is always a fun one to learn, and there will no doubt be lots of laughter at first, so this is a good one to save for the end of your warm-up routine!

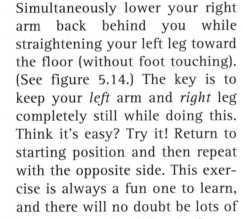

FIGURE 5.14
Dead bug

ENDURANCE

Now that your young athletes are strong and flexible, you're ready to incorporate the third element of conditioning, endurance training. But what kind? Basketball is a game of starts and stops. Rarely does

TO PLYO OR NOT TO PLYO? THAT IS THE QUESTION

A word on *plyometrics*. Plyometrics is a popular form of conditioning designed to increase explosiveness and jumping ability. Many people know its various forms, such as bounding, box jumps, depth jumps, cone hops. With very few exceptions, plyometric exercises should remain the province of older, physically mature athletes (high school age or older). Pre-adolescent athletes' bodies are still maturing, and their joints are ill prepared for the pounding that mid- to high-intensity plyometric programs involve. Nine-year-olds don't need to increase their vertical jump. They need to focus on dribbling head up and pivoting while balanced. Focus your teaching energies on the fundamentals.

the action go on for more than a minute or two at a time before play stops, however briefly, due to a turnover, a foul, or some other dead ball situation. Basketball is a game of *recovery time*. How efficiently will your players be able to catch their breath during the short breaks in the action? You want athletes to recover quickly during a stoppage in play, so that they are fresh and ready for the next flurry of action.

There is a well-worn phrase that goes, "Fatigue makes cowards of us all." Actually, I think it just makes us kind of dumb. Think about it: When you are exhausted, that is *all* you are able to focus on . . . how tired you are. Makes it rather difficult to think about much else, such as how to read a defender or fight over an on-ball pick. I've seen conditioning beat talent on many occasions.

Ideally, of course, your players will gain their conditioning through the drills you put them through and any scrimmage work you conduct at practice. Try to get your players to understand that the more they put into practice, the more they will get out of it. Make it a point not to use straight running as a conditioner. Involve the basketball or some sort of defensive technique in any conditioning drill so that they are learning while getting in shape. Here are some drills that I like:

Gill Drill

Named for Pam Gill-Fisher, former basketball coach at UC Davis, this is one of my favorites for young players. Easy to learn, it incorporates passing and catching while on the move with shooting. Passers occupy the six designated spots. There are two lines of players, each with a ball (preferably). The two lines are at each end of the court. The first player in line passes to the FT-line passer and sprints down-court. Taking a return pass, she immediately sends the ball to the sideline passer. The first player gets the return pass from the sideline passer and sends it ahead to the opposite FT-line passer. Finally, she gets one last return pass and dribbles in for a lay-up. (See figure 5.15.) The second person in line waits until the player ahead of her has received her *second* pass before starting. At intervals, the coach blows the whistle and six new players take the passing spots. It's basketball's version of musical chairs, and it can be a lot of fun. The players may not even realize they're getting in shape!

Continuous Lay-Ups

This can be done over any time interval (2:00, 3:00, 4:00). All you need are two balls, a shooting line, and an outlet line at each end. The shooter passes to the outlet receiver, who dribbles to the middle of the floor and toward the far basket. The shooter *sprints* to the out-

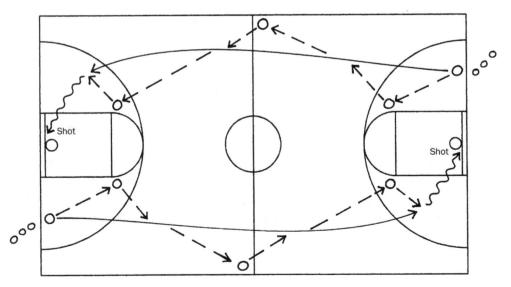

FIGURE 5.15
Gill drill

side lane and takes the return pass for a lay-up at the opposite basket. The next shooter at that end grabs the ball out of the basket and passes to the outlet receiver, and so on. (See figure 5.16.) The shooter rotates to the outlet line, and the passer to the shooting line. Keep track of total lay-ups made. When you have a good sense of what your players are capable of, set a goal, in terms of number of lay-ups made, each time. When your players become comfortable with this drill, have them switch directions halfway through so that they get a chance to shoot from both the left and right sides. If they're really good, they can even switch on the fly, with the outlet line racing across to the opposite sideline.

Lay-Ups and Jumpers

Each player has a ball. Use one line per basket (5–7 players per basket is a good number). The player passes to the coach and then streaks downcourt. The coach throws the ball long downcourt, and the shooter must run it down and then take the shot. She rebounds

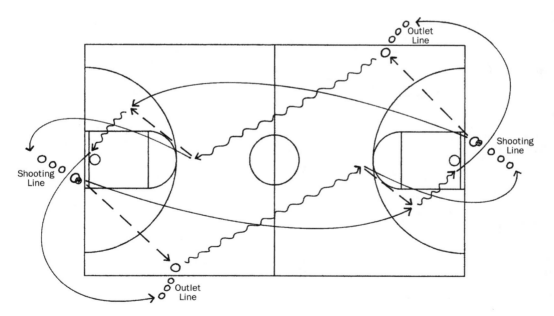

FIGURE 5.16
Continuous lay-ups

her own shot and passes to the coach at that end, streaking again back toward the basket where she started. Shoot lay-ups at the far basket, with short jump shots coming back. (See figure 5.17.) *Hint:* If you have sidecourts (the shorter courts that run sideways across the main court in the gym), split your squad evenly among these courts. The shorter court actually means your players will get in more shots in the time you allot for this drill.

Two-Ball Shooting

This is actually more of a conditioner for the rebounders than for the shooters. Assign three players and two balls per basket. The shooter goes "around the horn" and back, working her way back to the starting point and shooting from the five spots designated on the floor. Rebounders alternate rebounding shots and sprinting to place the ball on the floor at the next shooter's spot. (See figure 5.18.) Rebounders must get the ball down before the shooter arrives. Rotate shooters.

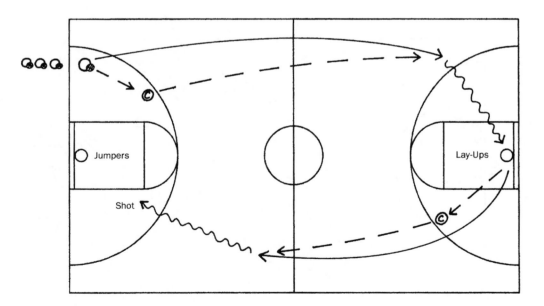

FIGURE 5.17
Lay-ups and jumpers

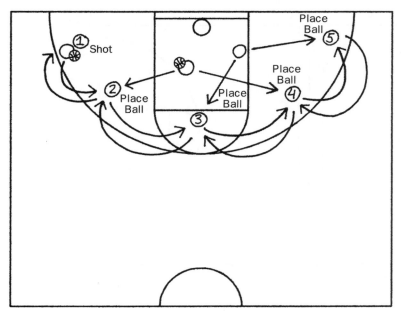

FIGURE 5.18
Two-ball shooting

Figure 8s

This is a follow-the-leader defensive footwork drill. Starting at one corner, the first player, followed closely by her teammates, will sprint to midcourt, defensive slide to far sideline, sprint to far baseline, backpedal to midcourt, use a defensive slide to the far sideline, and backpedal to baseline. (See figure 5.19.) The first few times you have them attempt this drill, have players go at about three-quarter speed. Emphasize technique and form on the defensive slides, staying low and not crossing their feet. As they get fatigued, they'll want to stand up and start loping along instead of sliding. Have them yell, "Ball, ball!" when in defensive slide, conditioning them to talk on defense.

There are obviously many ways to incorporate conditioning activities into your regular practice drills. Be creative. Stay imaginative. Stay positive. Continually emphasize how much stronger the players are getting. Assure them that no other team is working as hard as they are, and because of that, the fourth quarter of every

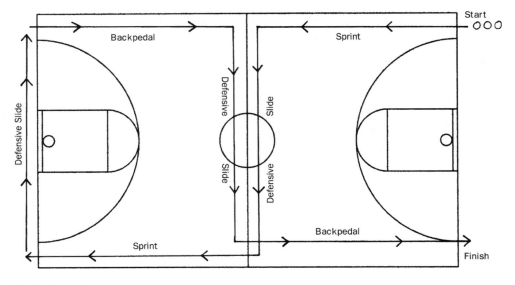

FIGURE 5.19
Figure 8s

game will be *theirs*. Reinforce how good they feel about themselves when they have completed a tough workout. But most of all, as with everything else you do with young kids, *make it fun for them and for yourself!*

6

PRACTICE PLANNING

BASKETBALL GAMES ARE generally not won or lost on the day of the contest. Most games are won during the week, at practice. It is preparation that largely determines a team's chances for success on game day. When you watch a team deftly handling every situation it encounters in a game, you are observing a team that has practiced well and efficiently over the course of that week. Teams that are "fundamentally sound" inevitably achieve that by repetition, practicing fundamental skills over and over again until they become instinctive.

Nowhere is the practice setting more important than in youth basketball. Young players are still learning the basic skills and tactics of the game. As a coach, your primary job is to teach these skills to your players in practice, allowing them to progress to the point at which they are confident when they attempt them in game situations. It takes time and patience, but if you didn't possess both attributes in abundance, you would not be coaching youth basketball, would you?

Approach practice planning with the three F's in mind. Your first emphasis should be on *fundamentals*. Teaching the game's basic skills should be your top priority. Most young players are not yet ready to understand or absorb intricate offensive or defensive patterns and systems. They're still learning to dribble, pass, and shoot.

Be devoted to developing those abilities. Second, be *flexible*. Even the best-planned practice sometimes requires modification, perhaps because of missing players or because a drill took longer than the time you allotted. Last, have *fun*. Remember: It's the journey, not the destination, that's most important. Try to make the process enjoyable. If you and your players have fun at practice, you will all get more out of them.

MASTER PLAN

Before you begin thinking about daily practice plans, look at the big picture. What do you want to accomplish over the course of the season? What do you want your players to learn? Sit down and draw up a master plan for the season. Think of it as a "teaching plan," a list of the instructional goals that you wish to accomplish. A sample plan for the youngest players might be:

- Players will learn the offensive "triple threat" position.
- Players will be able to pivot with either foot.
- Players will be able to dribble with either hand.
- Players will learn to throw chest and bounce passes.
- Players will know how to set effective screens for teammates.
- Players will learn how to V-cut and get themselves open.
- Players will learn proper defensive stance.
- Players will learn how to "slide" defensively when guarding the ballhandler.
- Players will learn how to defend off-ball.
- Players will be able to shoot right- and left-handed lay-ups.
- Players will learn proper shooting technique.

Obviously, the list can be extended *ad infinitum*. Your job is to decide which skills are most important for the age and skill level of your players. Don't make

Coaching Tip

Knowing how much time to devote to a drill is a skill acquired through experience. Many young coaches fail to allot enough time for drills, forcing them to cut an exercise short or eliminate a later drill. When this happens to you, note it on your practice plan. Later, calculate why the sequence ran long and modify the drill or set aside more time.

the mistake of trying to teach *everything.* It can't be done. Endeavor to teach a few things well rather than many things poorly.

Progressions

Think of the individual basketball skills as building blocks. First, you must build the foundation by teaching the fundamental skills, such as passing, pivoting, dribbling, catching, and shooting (see figure 6.1). Then, progress to the next level of skill development by combining two or more of the fundamentals in order to teach a new skill, such as passing off the dribble or catching a pass and shooting. These are called *progressions* and are the very heart of learning any physical activity. The basic premise is that if you ask players to perform a certain skill, be sure they have already learned the individual components that make up that skill.

Breakdowns

If progressions involve construction, or using fundamental skills as building blocks for more complex skills, *breakdowns* involve deconstruction, or breaking down the whole to discover its parts. Think of it

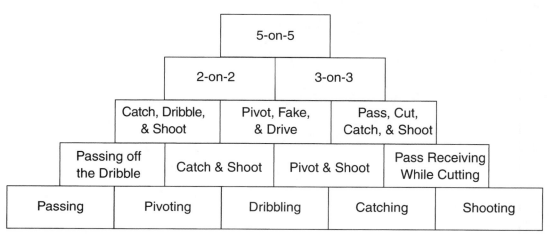

FIGURE 6.1
Sample progression chart

as using a reverse process to find the progressions you want to begin teaching with. For example, if you are introducing a basic flex offense to your team, examine the five-player motion, as in figure 6.2.

1. Break it down into drills involving *four* players (see figure 6.3).
2. Break it down into drills involving *three* players (see figure 6.4).
3. Break it down into drills involving *two* players (see figure 6.5).

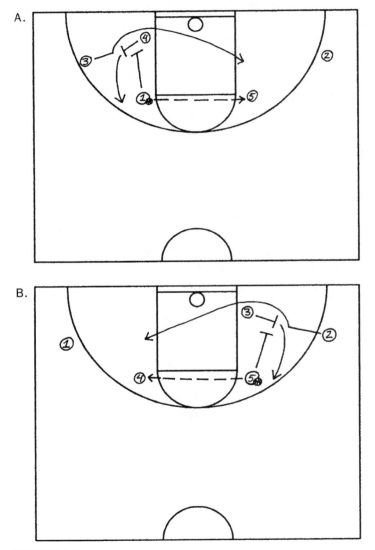

FIGURE 6.2
5-player motion

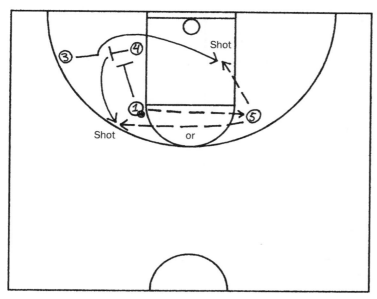

FIGURE 6.3
Flex breakdown: 4-player drill

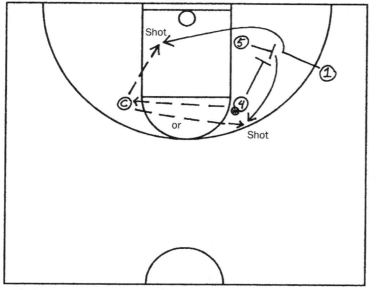

FIGURE 6.4
Flex breakdown: 3-player drill

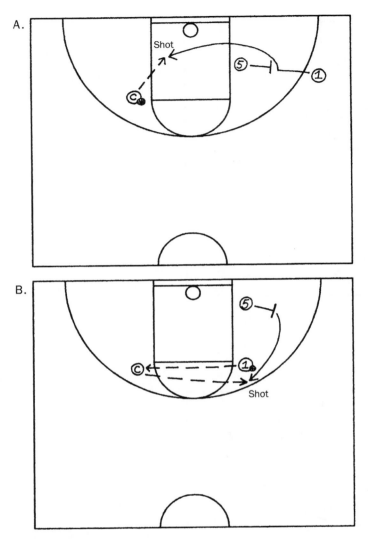

FIGURE 6.5
Flex breakdown: 2-player drill

Now that you have broken down the flex offense all the way to two-player interactions, reverse the process and begin building with the two-player drills. Eventually progress to three- and then four-player drills. Finally, now that your players have a firm grasp of the various components, you are ready to try a five-player motion. Make sure that your players understand the drills at each level before progressing to the next. You can break down *any* system using this method.

DAILY PRACTICE PLANS

Once you have a master plan in place, it's time to plan your daily practices. Take the necessary time to prepare and organize in advance. For many youth teams, practice time is limited. The more organized you are, the more effective your practices will be. If you try to wing it, you'll experience frequent dead spots in practice while you try to decide what to do next. Meanwhile, your players will be standing around, getting bored, and losing energy.

Coaching Tip

Breakdown drills are little more than a series of drills in which players work on fundamental offensive and defensive skills. They are valuable because they relate *specifically* to some larger offensive or defensive framework. If players master breakdown drills, they will have all the tools and materials necessary to "build" your system.

What makes for a good practice? Here are some general considerations:

- **Be organized.** Have a purpose in mind. Know what you want to accomplish when you take the floor.
- **Keep the pace brisk.** Young players, in particular, have short attention spans. Change activities often, keeping drill segments short and snappy.
- **Use progressions.** Spend a large percentage of your practice time on fundamentals.
- **Use competitive drills.** Children love contests, and making drills competitive helps keep them attentive and enthusiastic. Reward, if you wish, but don't punish.
- **Keep everyone involved.** Avoid having too many players standing around. If you have the staff to manage it, break into smaller groups whenever possible and give each player as much on-court time as possible.

- **Be positive and upbeat.** Remember: Enthusiasm is contagious. Praise far more often than you criticize. Keep the atmosphere fun!

Laying out a daily practice schedule is like putting together a puzzle. You may have fifteen different segments planned, each designed to address a certain area of the game (shooting, rebounding, defense). But how much time do you give to each segment? And in what order do you conduct the drills? Well, figuring that out is part of the fun.

DRILL TO PERFECTION

Many coaches use drills that we have borrowed from other coaches we admire. On the other hand, part of the fun of coaching is devising new drills to suit our own needs. But whether by larceny or creativity, we are always searching for a better way to do things. What constitutes a "good" drill?

- **Brevity.** Use 5 to 7 minutes maximum for individual skill development. You may occasionally allot more time for "team" drills since you are trying to coordinate more players at a given time.

- **Competitiveness.** Not always, but often. Competitive drills, used judiciously, with something (either a reward or penalty avoidance) at stake can keep your players working at a high intensity level while having fun. It also gives you an opportunity to observe which players on your team relish competition for its own sake (not all will). Used too frequently, however, competition in practice may become anxiety producing for some of your players.

- **Conditioning.** A good drill should be executed with high intensity and should contribute to the players' physical conditioning. Of course, some of that depends on the particular player's work ethic.

- **Small groups.** The fewer the number of players at any given drill station, the more practice each will get. Eliminate idleness.

- **Progression.** Early season drills will most often isolate fundamental skills. Later drills may focus on a series of interrelated skills.

- **Player decisions.** The more often players are faced with decision-making scenarios, the sooner they will develop their "court sense" and be equipped to handle situations that come up during games.

How much time you devote to each drill depends on the drill itself and how strongly you wish to emphasize it that particular day. If the drill is a new one that you haven't used before, you may need to teach it a few times before you get a sense of what the optimum time allotment will be. Strive to spend exactly the amount of time you deem necessary, no more, no less. Don't get locked into planning practice in 5- or 10-minute blocks. For some drills, 7 minutes may be perfect. For others, 4 minutes may be enough. And resist the temptation to drag out a drill if the players are struggling with it.

Coaching Tip

In searching for the perfect drill, you may have to give a little so that you can best achieve your goal. When introducing an inbounds play, you may have to talk players through all possible situations. Accept that conditioning will not be a part of this practice segment.

You'll want to stick with it until they get it right, but you're better off staying on schedule, moving to the next drill, and redressing the poorly executed drill at the next practice.

Make variety your guide when piecing together a practice. Don't fall into a stale routine by practicing the same things in the same order every time you take the floor. For example, some days you might practice team defense near the end of practice. On others, you'll practice team defense early on, when your players are fresh. Free throws should sometimes, but not always, be scheduled following a conditioning drill so players can learn to shoot while fatigued. Over many years of planning practices, I've learned that there's a certain art in establishing the right tempo and flow and pace. Planning the perfect practice may be impossible, but the fun is in trying. Perfection aside, following is a sample practice plan for a more advanced youth team.

Keep in mind that your practices will only be as good as the effort you put into planning them. You want your players to play hard and have fun. The better prepared you are and the more organized your practices are, the more you can focus on your team's effort and development rather than wondering what to do next. To paraphrase a popular coaching sentiment: It's not the will to win that distinguishes great teams; it's the will to *prepare* to win.

Practice Plan

4:00–4:05	**Free Shooting**	**BLUE:** Olivia/Jennifer/Kara/Shawna/ Madison/ Chelsea
		WHITE: Brittney/Sherida/Nancy/Maria/ Jorja/Chrissy
		Goal for today: TALK on defense
4:06–4:10	**Full-Court Lay-ups**	
4:11–4:20	**Offensive Stations**	4 players per basket
		Rotate every 3 minutes
		Basket #1: Bank shots
		Basket #2: Dribbling
		Basket #3: Bounce passes
4:21–4:26	**Free Throws**	Shoot 10 free throws, then rotate
4:27–4:33	**Individual Defense**	On-ball and off-ball (3 minutes each)
4:34–4:41	**4-on-4 SHELL Defense**	Emphasize making ballhandler dribble toward baseline
		BLUE: Shawna/Chelsea/Madison/Nancy
		WHITE: Olivia/Brittney/Jennifer/Chrissy
		RED: Sherida/Maria/Jorja/Kara
4:42–4:47	**3-on-2 Full Court**	
4:48–4:53	**5-Spot Shooting**	3 players per basket
4:54–4:59	**Free Throws**	Shoot 2, then rotate. Total of 10.
5:00–5:04	**Rebounding**	
5:05–5:15	**Team Offense**	
5:16–5:25	**Scrimmage 5-on-5**	
5:26–5:30	**Shooting Relay**	
5:30	**Practice Ends**	

Announcements

1. Game Friday at 4:00 P.M. @ Silveyville
2. Pizza after Silveyville game
3. Happy Birthday, Olivia!
4. Next practice: Monday, 5:00–6:30 P.M.

7

SHOOTING

IF THERE'S ONE thing that all basketball players love to practice, it's shooting. The point of the game, after all, is to *score*. So motivating your players to practice their shooting should be child's play.

The problem is, if someone practices the wrong technique, instead of getting better, she only reinforces poor mechanics. This problem is especially acute for young players, who are still growing and developing coordination and physical strength. Younger players are often not strong enough to get the ball to the basket (particularly if the basket height is non-adjustable) without putting their whole body into the shot, resulting in the ball being "thrown," as opposed to shot. As the players mature and become strong enough to shoot the ball properly, they often have to unlearn poor shooting habits as they strive to learn proper technique.

When a player is learning a new skill or is practicing a skill differently, it feels awkward at first because her muscles are being used in a different manner. She may experience some muscle soreness for the same reason. When youngsters are first practicing a new skill, they should stop when their muscles fatigue. If not, their form will suffer, and they'll begin reinforcing poor habits.

Gradually increase practice time each day as players' muscles adapt and build endurance. This is the process of teaching muscle memory. Shooting must become instinctive. Except on free throws,

Coaching Tip

With your foot pointed straight toward the hoop, swing your right arm freely at your side. Now, pronate your right foot slightly inward and swing your arm again. Your right arm can no longer swing freely. It keeps banging against your hip because it wants to "follow" your right toe's alignment to the left of the basket.

there is no time to "think" about the proper shooting form. The players must "feel" it. Becoming a great shooter means practicing properly until it becomes a reflexive action.

When starting out, your players should stay within their comfortable shooting range and resist the temptation to shoot from farther out too soon. Doing so may cause them to strain and alter their form so that they are no longer practicing the correct technique. When, and only when, their form is solid on the stationary shot should they practice shots off the move: jump shots off the dribble, catch-and-shoot, and the like.

Shooting has two primary components: *mechanics* (alignment and form) and *judgment* (shot selection).

MECHANICS

If you were to gather ten of the WNBA's best players together and watched each of their shots, you would see ten slightly varying styles. Shooting forms are like snowflakes—no two are exactly alike. However, almost all good shooters do three things well:

1. They keep their shooting elbows in, or "square"
2. They extend up and shoot with good arc on the ball
3. They snap their wrists on the follow-through

And of those three, the last is the most important. A good wrist release can turn many ugly duckling shots into beautiful swans.

Let's take a good look at the important mechanics involved in a solid shooting form:

1. **Torso.** Designate a shooting side and a balance side. The shooting side for a right-hander would obviously be the right, with the left comprising the balance side.

2. **Feet.** Aim the lead, or shooting, foot at the center of the basket, straight on (see Coaching Tip above). This will keep the hips square. Don't

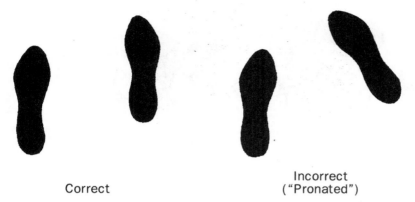

Correct

Incorrect
("Pronated")

FIGURE 7.1
Correct and incorrect foot position when shooting

turn the foot in (pronate). Your trail, or balance, foot can face any direction, but it should be approximately shoulder-width apart and have a toe-to-instep relationship to the right foot. See figure 7.1 for examples of correct and incorrect foot position.

3. Knees. Flex knees just enough to raise heels slightly off the floor.

4. Elbows. Line up the point of the shooting elbow with the center of the lead foot (see figure 7.2). This will keep the elbow in (very important) even if it wants to fly out to the right. The height of the elbow depends on the age and strength of the player (see figure 7.3). The younger the player, the lower she'll need to start her shot to generate enough power to reach the basket. A *low set-up* places the elbow at belly level and allows for a maximum push up and through to the basket. A *medium set-up* places the elbow at shoulder level or slightly below, allowing the shooter to sight the basket over the top of the ball. A *high set-up* places the elbow at chin-to-nose level. The high set-up is ideal for employing shot-fakes. By holding the ball higher, it is more difficult for the defender to block the shot. However, only those players who are physically strong will be able to reach the basket from a high set-up.

FIGURE 7.2
Shooting elbow aligned over lead foot

Low   Medium   High

FIGURE 7.3
Elbow height on shot set-up

5. Wrist. Keep the back of the hand parallel to the floor. This allows the shooter to push *up* and through the ball, not *out* and through. As a result, the shooter is better able to keep the shot's trajectory, or arc, high (see figure 7.4). If the wrist is *overcocked*, the shooter will feel strain in her forearm and inevitably shoot short. If the wrist is *undercocked*, the shooter will tend to shoot flat. Still, it's better to be undercocked than overcocked. Most important, emphasize pushing *up* and *through* the ball.

FIGURE 7.4
Proper wrist position

6. Grip. Rest the ball on the finger *pads* (not finger-*tips*) of both hands, with the shooting hand slightly behind and slightly underneath the ball. If the ball is setting on the palm, spread the fingers *slightly* to bring the ball up off the palm and on to the finger pads. The side of the thumb rests on the ball. Otherwise, the thumb will kick through and influence the direction of the ball. As the ball comes up to the ready position, the index and middle finger should be aligned *directly* in front of or over the shooting shoulder. The balance hand should be placed on the side of ball. Do not obstruct vision: *Both* eyes are needed to judge distance. Sight through the triangle formed by the forearm if the elbow is in a medium or high position. Sight over the top of the ball if the elbow is in a low position.

Coaching Tip

To get a good sense of where the finger pads are, slap the ball back and forth in your hands several times. Red or stinging areas will be where the ball should rest.

7. **Release.** As you begin your shot and your legs extend, release the ball by pushing up and through with the shooting elbow, extending up (not *out*) toward the basket.

8. **Arc.** There are three types of shooting trajectories (see figure 7.5). With *low* arc (also known as shooting "flat"), the ball can enter only the back portion of the basket because of the angle. So the shooter is giving away at least one-third of her target. *High* arc requires too much physical effort and is therefore inefficient. *Medium* arc is the most efficient and gives the shooter the best possible chance for success. It's similar to the choices Goldilocks was presented with: too low, too high, and *just right!*

9. **Follow-through.** The hand should *snap* through either straight over the top of the basket or slightly pronated to the outside (see figure 7.6). The two lead fingers (index and middle) will be slightly lower and closer to the floor than the two outside fingers. If following-through is to the inside, the two outside fingers will be lower. The ball will come off the index and middle fingers last. Push *up* (extend) and *snap* the wrist on the follow-through. Don't shoot out *at* the basket. Backspin rotation should be gentle. The ball shouldn't be spinning wildly, quickly, or sideways.

The two most common problems you'll find with shooters of all ages are an "inside" follow-through with the hand and wrist (see "Incorrect" method in figure 7.6) and a lack of arc on the shot (see figure 7.5). If a player is shooting the ball straight, but is missing long and short, there's really nothing seriously wrong. It's simply a matter of making slight adjustments (getting more lift from the legs, adding a little more arc, snapping the follow-through). If a player is

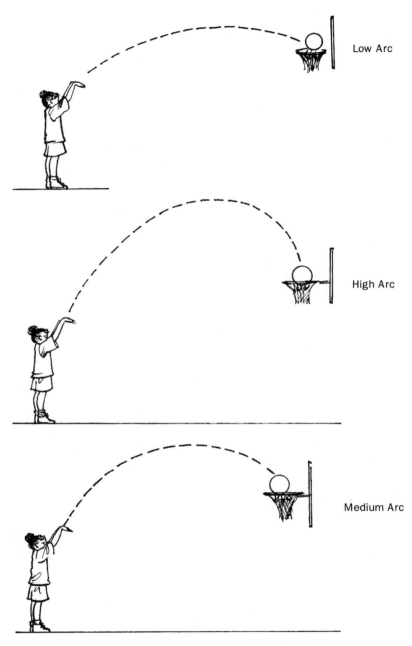

Low Arc

High Arc

Medium Arc

FIGURE 7.5
Three types of shooting trajectories

Correct   Correct   Incorrect

FIGURE 7.6
Correct and incorrect follow-through

missing left or right consistently, then there are some alignment problems that need addressing.

Shot Charting

Here's a good way to determine what, if any, areas of your players' mechanics need addressing. For each player, draw 100 circles on a piece of paper. Each circle represents a basket rim. Have each player shoot 100 shots in her range from straight on to the basket. She should shoot from the same spot each time. Make a note on her chart where each shot initially hits on the rim, whether it is a successfully made shot or a missed attempt. If the made shot is a swish (a shot that enters the basket cleanly, not touching the rim), place an *S* inside the circle to denote it. An *M* denotes any other make and should be placed where the ball initially hits the rim. An *X* shows any miss and

VIDEOTAPING THE SHOT

One of the best ways to make certain that your players' mechanics are solid is to videotape them shooting. If possible, film the shots from three different angles. Here's what to look for from each spot:

From behind:

    a. Knees flexed

    b. Index and middle finger of shooting hand aligned over shoulder

    c. Rotation of ball (backspin)

From the side:

    a. Wrist cocked (back of shooting hand parallel to the floor)

    b. Push up and through, not out

From the front:

    a. Eyes remain on target; don't follow ball

    b. Balance hand not obstructing or impeding shot

    c. Elbow in and aligned over shooting toe

    d. Follow-through pronated or straight; index and middle fingers "lower" than last two fingers

should also be placed where the ball initially hits the rim. Figure 7.7 shows a sample shot charting form with one row filled in.

Examine the marks for each player to see if a pattern emerges. Too many back rim hits probably means the player is shooting too flat. She should shoot up and put more arc on the ball. Lots of front rim shots means the player either is not using her legs or is not snapping her follow-through. If a player misses right or left, it'll likely be mostly all one side or the other. For right-handers, missing left can result from any number of things: following through to the inside (two fingers low); feet aligned improperly, which turns hips to the left (Is the right foot pronated inward?); and so on. Missing to the right consistently probably means that either a player's left foot is not in a toe-to-instep relationship with her right and is somehow sneaking in front of her right foot. This aligns the hips to the right, which causes

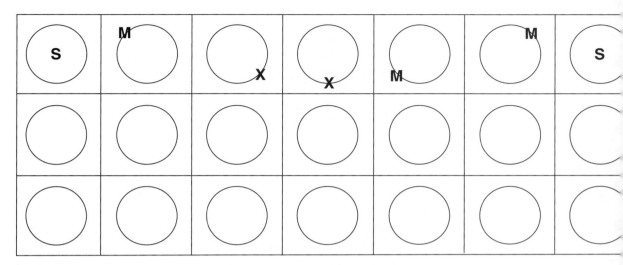

FIGURE 7.7
Shot charting

the shoulders to do the same, and a domino effect ensues. The other possibility is that the player is bringing the ball up to the ready position across her body from left to right, and the momentum carries into her release.

JUDGMENT

Having a good grasp of shooting mechanics is important, but great technique needs to be accompanied by sound shooting *judgment*. By this I mean that a great shooter not only knows *how* to shoot, but also knows *when* to shoot. What is a good shot? It's when a player is in her range, is not too tightly defended, and no teammate has a better shot. The last point is the most important. No shot is a good shot if a teammate has an easier, more makeable opportunity. If a potential shooter is being so closely defended that she has to "force" her shot to get it off, then *that* is not a good shot. That leaves the third component of shooting judgment, being within range. In other words, is the player close enough to the basket to easily reach the hoop?

To determine range, have each player start underneath the basket with a *bank* shot. Have her shoot, take one step back, shoot another bank shot, take one step back, and so on, until it becomes a strain to reach the target. The point where it becomes a strain marks the boundary of that player's range. Just because a player can *reach* the basket doesn't mean she's in her range.

Bank Shots

"Bank" shots, or shots that carom off the backboard before entering the basket (also known as shooting off "the glass"), allow for the greatest margin of error when used from certain spots on the floor. If a shot is slightly off line, the backboard helps "correct" the shot before directing it to the hoop. Bank shots should be used often when the shooter is comfortably within her range and is inside the "bank funnel" (see figure 7.8). The ball should "kiss" (or carom gently off) the backboard on the *downward* trajectory. The softer the angle, or the closer to the baseline a player is, the more she'll need to aim to

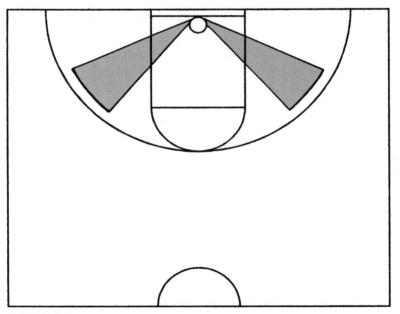

FIGURE 7.8
Bank shot funnels

the outside of the target square painted on the backboard.

Free Throws

Good free-throw shooters have a routine they go through while standing at the line. It might be *dribble three times, spin the ball, index finger on the logo, sight the target, then let it fly.* Whatever it may be, encourage your players to develop a routine that they're comfortable with and stick with it. The free throw is an uncontested shot, so players know they won't have to rush or change their release because of a strong defender. It comes down to a matter of concentration and focus.

Coaching Tip

When practicing shooting, try to practice moving at "game speed." Many players practice shooting at about half-speed, moving without hurry from one spot to another. When they get in a game, they have to move faster and shoot more quickly, and they haven't really practiced at that speed.

When you have your team practice free throws, vary the routine for your players. Although shooting ten or twenty free throws in a row may help them develop a rhythm, it's not realistic; you would never shoot that many consecutively in a game. Sometimes have them only shoot one or two before rotating. Create "pressure" situations for them. Have them shoot immediately following a conditioning drill, when they're likely to be fatigued, just as they might be during a game. Mix it up, and you will see your players' shooting percentages rise dramatically.

Lay-ups

The lay-up is, theoretically, the highest percentage shot you can get. However, many young players struggle with this shot, so it is a good idea to work on it with your team.

Taking off close to the basket, the shooter wants to jump explosively by planting the foot opposite her shooting hand while driving the knee of her shooting side up toward the basket. At the top of the

FIGURE 7.9
Lay-up

jump, the player will release the shot toward the back-board (*always* encourage her to use the backboard on lay-ups). See figure 7.9. Teach your players to shoot with both their right and left hands.

Remember that different players have varying apti-tudes for different physical activities. Shooting a basket-ball is no different. Some players seem to be naturals, while many others struggle to find any level of consis-tency. Not every young girl will develop the feathery touch of a Sheryl Swoopes or a Jackie Stiles. But we are *all* capable of maximizing our potential for a given skill. Anyone can become a "better" shooter. All it takes is hard work, dedication, hard work, proper techniques, and hard work!

8

TEACHING FUNDAMENTAL SKILLS

As YOU SIT down to plan your first few practices, one of your first questions will be, "What skills do I want my players to learn?" The master plan you developed for your team in chapter 6 will give you a list of the skills you want to impart. Your next question is, "Where do I begin?" Now *that* is a good question! Your impulse may well be to try to teach everything in the first several practices. Resist that impulse! Understand that it is impossible to cover every aspect of the game, even over the course of an entire season, much less in a few practices. But you can begin to build your players' understanding of the game and their grasp of the fundamental skills beginning with your first workout.

Deciding what to cover depends on the skill level of your players. Most youth teams have a wide range of abilities among their players, and one of your most delicate tasks will be to teach to *all* skill levels. You don't want to hold your most skilled players back, but you don't want your novice players to feel completely lost either.

Start with the most basic skills, and use progressions to move on to the more complex skills involved in the game. The legendary John Wooden, who coached UCLA to ten NCAA national championships and who was fortunate to coach some of the most talented players in collegiate history, began every season by teaching his players the most efficient way to tie their shoelaces! In addition, throughout the season he would have his players begin practice with the most rudimentary pivoting, dribbling, and passing drills. He believed in the basics, and he reinforced that belief in his players daily.

Your basic rule of thumb is this: When asking your players to execute a skill or drill, be sure that they have a grasp of all the fundamental skills that will be used in that drill. For example, if you conduct a simple team lay-up drill, your players should be able to dribble, jump stop, throw a bounce pass, catch a bounce pass, and shoot a lay-up. You should have worked on all these areas before asking them to integrate their skills for this drill.

For youth basketball players, a majority of your practice time should be devoted to fundamental skill development in the following areas:

- Footwork
- Ball handling
- Dribbling
- Passing
- Individual offense
- Individual defense (on- and off-ball)
- Shooting

That's a lot to cover in the sometimes short time span allotted to youth league teams. But the time you spend teaching a half-court team offense will be wasted if your players cannot execute the components that comprise it. Even for advanced players, reinforcement of fundamental skills is a good idea.

OFFENSIVE SKILLS

Triple-Threat Position

The triple-threat position is the foundation of offensive basketball. Almost all other offensive skills originate from this position. Triple threat means that a player is able to (1) pass, (2) drive (dribble), or (3) shoot, all from a single position or stance facing the basket. This keeps the defense honest, as they cannot predict what the offensive player might do. If, on the other hand, a player catches the ball and tries to protect it from the defender by turning her back to the basket, she is no longer a threat to shoot or drive aggressively (she would have to turn back to face the basket to do either), and it would be difficult to pass to anyone near the basket. This makes the defender's job much easier.

Being on-balance is one of the most important attributes in basketball. Every skill a player tries to execute should start from a balanced position. In general, this means an equal weight distribution between both feet. If you were to set down two bathroom scales and have a player place a foot on each scale, the readout should be the same for both feet. Balance gives a player the opportunity to go in any direction (or straight up!) without adjustment.

To assume the triple-threat position, a player should stand with her feet slightly wider than her hips and on-balance. Knees should be slightly bent. The player should be slightly bent over at the waist. She should hold the ball as she would grip it when shooting, not out in front, but back toward one hip, forcing the defender to reach in off-balance if she wishes to attempt a steal. (See figure 8.1.) From this position, the player is ready to pass to an open teammate, drive to the basket if the defender is out of position, or pull up and shoot if the defender plays too far off.

FIGURE 8.1
Triple-threat position

Footwork

Once players have a grasp of the triple-threat position and a sense of being balanced, you can begin work on footwork and pivoting. Remember that there are ten players on the floor at any given moment, and only one has the ball. That leaves nine players, four on offense and five on defense, who need to be able to move without the ball. Thus, footwork is essential to good basketball because players will spend about 80–90 percent of the game *without* the ball.

Pivoting

Being able to pivot is essential in both defensive and offensive play, but particularly in the latter. Pivoting is simply a matter of stopping and then turning with one foot forward (front pivot) or backward

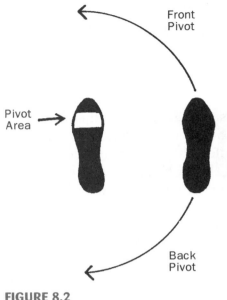

Front
Pivot

Pivot
Area

Back
Pivot

FIGURE 8.2
Pivoting

(reverse pivot), while keeping the other foot (usually the ball of the foot) on the floor at all times. (See figure 8.2.) The pivot is most frequently used by the ballhandler to remain mobile and elusive from a defender without committing a traveling violation. Once the ballhandler has established her pivot foot, or the foot kept in contact with the floor at all times, she may not change it during that particular possession.

When working on pivoting, players should be instructed to stay low at all times. Many beginning players stand up during the pivot motion and crouch back down at the completion of the turn. Ideally, the head remains level throughout the motion.

Pivoting can be one of the trickiest moves for young players to master. While they may have the technique down, when faced with defensive pressure, many youngsters instinctively stand up, turn their backs to the bas-

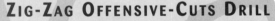

ZIG-ZAG OFFENSIVE-CUTS DRILL

The *zig-zag* is a popular basketball drill used to teach an assortment of footwork skills. Have your players form several lines of three to four players at one end of the court. Players jog at a 45-degree angle for a few steps, then plant with their outside foot and push off in the opposite direction, with their "free" foot leading the way. They should push off with their left foot if they wish to go right, and vice versa. Players should stay low when cutting, and cuts should be explosive. Have players cut 7–8 times as they run down the length of the court. *Common error:* Many players will plant with the inside leg and cross over with their outside leg to change direction (plant their left foot to cut back to the left). Work slowly at the start so that your players can master the technique.

ket, and then, in an effort to get away from the pressure, change or drag their pivot foot. Players who have a good concept of the triple-threat position are less susceptible because they are in a position to drive if a defender plays too tight (assuming they have not yet picked up their dribble).

Cutting

Cutting involves the ability to change direction on the court, both defensively and offensively. Getting open on offense and responding to an opposing offensive player's move on defense are both predicated on being balanced and being able to change direction instantly.

The three primary offensive cuts in basketball are the V-cut, the L-cut, and the basket (backdoor) cut. On the V-cut, in particular, make certain that players cut back for the ball on a different line than they used for setting up their defender. Cutting back-and-forth on the same line is called an *I-cut* for the letter the cutter's path resembles. It rarely gets the player open unless she is infinitely quicker than the defender. The ideal cut looks more like the letter "V," setting up the defender on one path and cutting back toward the ball on another. (See figure 8.3.) Unfortunately, the I-cut is the one your players will use 99 percent of the time initially. Be patient and keep working with them. It's a thrill for you both when they finally get the hang of it.

The L-cut and the "basket-cut" are used less frequently but can be very effective when used properly. The L-cut involves taking the defender toward the ball and then cutting out to the side at

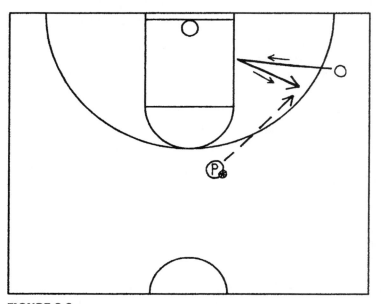

FIGURE 8.3
V-cut

a 90-degree angle to receive the pass. (See figure 8.4.) This is a very effective way to get open, but requires more precise timing between the passer and receiver than does the V-cut. The basket-cut is sometimes called the "backdoor cut" because rather than coming away from the basket to receive the pass, the offensive player cuts *to* the basket to catch the ball. (See figure 8.5.) This is most commonly used when a defender is cutting off the passing lane too aggressively (see "Denial Defense" later in this chapter) and gets caught out of position away from the basket. This may provide the opportunity for the offensive player to cut hard back toward the basket, leaving the defender trailing.

Ball Handling

We will differentiate here between *ball handling* (the art of catching the basketball and then protecting it prior to passing, dribbling, or shooting) and *dribbling.* The two terms are sometimes used interchangeably by basketball coaches.

Young players need plenty of time to practice getting used to the feel of the basketball. You see some young gym rats carrying a basketball with them everywhere they go. These players will always have an advantage over their counterparts, because the ball will always feel *comfortable* to them. Encourage your players to work on their ball handling skills while away from practice.

Kids *love* to try ball-handling tricks. There will be plenty of laughter as they try things and fumble the ball. Be sensitive to the players who may feel frustration, and encourage them to spend more time on the basic ball-handling drills until they're ready to progress.

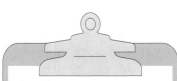

Coaching Tip

Teach players to keep eyes focused ahead, to hold the ball with finger pads, and to be bilateral (do everything with *both* hands). Many young players practice only with their strong or "good" hand. Encourage them to work extra hard on their weaker hand so defenders cannot overplay them.

Pass Receiving

Catching the variety of passes (good and bad) that a player sees over the course of a game is an art in itself. You'll constantly hear of this player or that

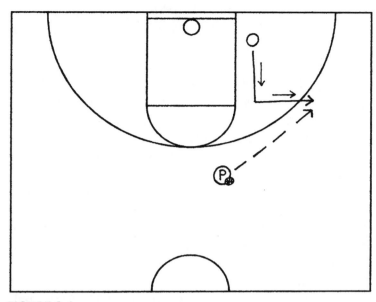

FIGURE 8.4
L-cut

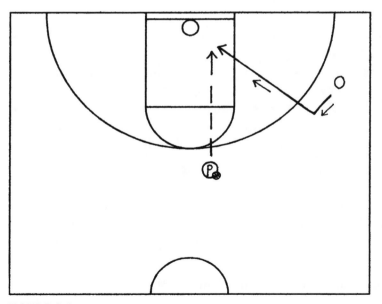

FIGURE 8.5
Basket cut

Coaching Tip

When working on ball handling and dribbling, it's a good sign if players make mistakes. It means they are exploring their limits. When a mistake happens, ask them to slow down and then push the envelope again once they're ready. If they never make a mistake, they're playing it too safe.

one having "good" or "soft" hands. This means they catch the ball well. But there's a lot more than having good hands that goes into catching the ball.

Any offensive player without the basketball should be moving around the court with her hands up at all times. Being surprised by a pass means either the player wasn't looking for the ball or she didn't have her hands ready to receive the ball. Players should always come to meet (move toward) the pass. This gives the defense less opportunity to deflect the ball, which can make the ball very difficult to catch. Players should give a target, offering an outstretched hand and letting her teammate know where she wants the ball. Finally, the receiver should catch the ball with both hands whenever possible.

If a player is having trouble catching the ball, it may be that she is taking her eyes off the ball too soon. Advise your player to "look" the ball into her hands. Another potential prob-

BALLHANDLING EXERCISES

Following are a series of exercises (some simple, some advanced) that your players can practice whenever they have enough room to swing a cat and there are no priceless artifacts in range. Players should start each exercise slowly and gradually build speed as they grow more confident. Remember to tell players to do each of these drills (where applicable) in *both* directions.

1. Move the ball in a circular motion around the head, waist, and ankles.

2. With arms fully extended, use wrists to quickly bat the ball back and forth between hands. Do this out in front and above the head.

3. Move the ball first around both legs, then around the right leg, and then around the left leg.

4. Move the ball around the legs in a figure-eight motion.

CONFIDENCE BUILDER

Here is a fun drill to help instill confidence at catching passes. Have a player stand with her back to the passer. Have the passer call out a teammate's name as she passes the ball. The receiver must jump and turn to catch the oncoming ball. Believe me, they will be concentrating *totally* on the ball! Most receivers will be a little nervous at first, but if you start by passing slowly and with enough time for them to react, they will begin to build confidence. As they grow more skilled, have passers start to pass the ball high or low, right or left, or any combination thereof. Have them pass earlier to give the receiver less reaction time. Test their limits! The only absolute rule? *Never* pass toward the face!

lem may be that she is tense and is fighting the ball. This can be harder to correct. Just keep encouraging her to relax and let the ball come to her. And, yes, I know that earlier I advised players to come meet every pass, but when tension is the problem, it's better, for a while at least, to have the player slow down and not press.

5. With legs apart, hold the ball with the right hand in front of the legs and the left hand behind. Drop the ball and let it bounce. Switch hands front to back and catch the ball. Repeat several times, switching hands.

6. Same drill as #5, but catch the ball *before* it bounces.

7. Same drill as #5, but hold the ball with both hands in front. Drop the ball and let it bounce. Switch both hands to behind you and catch the ball. Repeat several times, moving hands front to back and back to front.

8. Same drill as #7, but catch the ball *before* it bounces.

9. Throw the ball up in the air and catch it with two hands behind your back.

10. Pass the ball back and forth between your legs as you walk. Progress to running.

Dribbling

Dribbling is the most instinctive basketball skill to youngsters. Think about it. What happens when you hand a ball to a child? They immediately bounce it! Of course, *bouncing* a ball and *dribbling* a basketball are related only in the same sense that playing the scales and performing a concerto are both considered music.

Dribbling is an important basketball skill, but it's also the most overused. Many young players begin to dribble as soon as they receive a pass and don't take the time to look and evaluate the opportunities available to them. Encourage your players to slow down and consider passing before dribbling. That said, dribbling can be an effective way to move the ball around the court or to put pressure on the defense by driving to the basket and forcing a help situation, thus opening up a teammate.

To be an effective dribbler, technique must be developed, and most younger players have some built-in bad habits to overcome. The most common problems for young dribblers are:

1. Standing too upright while dribbling
2. "Slapping" at the ball rather than controlling the dribble with their finger pads
3. Watching the ball while they dribble

Help your players understand these principles of dribbling:

- Dribbling is a tactile skill. It is *not* visual. Keep the head up. Establish a feel for the ball; control it with the finger pads.
- Dribble primarily with the wrist and forearm. Using the shoulder results in a too-high dribble.
- The more closely guarded the player is, the lower she must dribble.
- Protect the ball with the body and off-arm (the one not being used for dribbling).
- Learn to dribble effectively with each hand.
- Be on-balanced and under control.
- Push the ball out in front when running.
- Keep changing pace and speed. Don't let a defender get into a rhythm with you.

DRIBBLING TIPS

When teaching dribbling skills, be sure to teach your players what they should be thinking and what they should be avoiding.

Think:

1. Dribble with a purpose. *Go* somewhere with your dribble.

2. Know what you want to do with the ball (shoot or pass) before you pick up the dribble.

3. Keep your head up so you can see the court.

Avoid:

1. Don't put the ball on the floor reflexively. Get into triple-threat position and evaluate first.

2. Don't be fancy when simple will do.

3. Don't force the dribble into defensive traffic. It's better to pull up too early than too late.

For players to gain a comfort level with dribbling the basketball, it's a good idea to limit movement at first. Let them try some things from a stationary position before you have them move up and down the court. Here are some good exercises (all should be done with head up and eyes forward, though at first the players should be given some leeway):

1. Kneeling on the left knee, dribble the ball with the right hand, emphasizing the motion with the wrist and forearm. Switch hands. Then bounce the ball back and forth under the right leg, alternating hands.

2. Sitting down, bounce the ball on the right side. Switch sides.

3. Standing up, dribble the ball in a figure-eight motion around and between the legs.

4. Dribble the ball back and forth in front of the body, from right to left and back, alternating hands.

5. Dribble the ball between the legs while walking.

There are several different types of dribbles that can be used in a variety of situations. But for young players, the emphasis should be on being able to do just two or three different types of dribble, but with either hand! It doesn't matter how many varieties of dribble a player learns if she does them all poorly or with just one hand. For the sake of providing options, however, let's discuss six basic dribbles, in decreasing order of importance.

1. **Control dribble.** This is the basic dribble to use when being closely guarded. Dribble close to the body and low (knee level) to the floor. Control ball with finger pads. Stay low and protect ball with off-arm.

2. **Speed dribble.** Used when sprinting down the court, this involves dribbling the ball higher and pushing it out in front. For some, alternating hands with each dribble increases the speed at which they can move.

3. **Crossover dribble.** Used for a change of direction. Dribbling hand flicks the ball very low and at about a 45-degree angle to the opposite hand, which continues the dribble. Trail foot (initial dribbling side) comes forward as body turns to protect the ball.

4. **Pull-back dribble.** Used when dribbler gets into traffic and needs to back up. Many players who get in trouble simply pick up the dribble and get stranded. On the pull-back, the dribbling hand moves in front of the ball and pulls back or dribbles the ball back toward body. All the time, the dribbler is shuffling backward to escape the defender. This dribble is often followed immediately with a crossover dribble to create more room to maneuver.

5. **Change-of-pace dribble.** This involves simply varying the height of the dribble or the rhythm and speed of the dribble to keep the defender off balance.

6. **Reverse (spin) dribble.** While dribbling, the dribbler reverses pivot and cups (places hand on the far side of the ball) the ball, pulling the ball back and around to the opposite side. She keeps the dribble alive with her new hand. For most young players, this dribble is difficult to execute without carrying the ball.

Passing

Passing is the most effective way to move the ball around the court. A passed ball can move from Point A to Point B faster than even the quickest player. Teams that pass the ball well will create many scoring opportunities for themselves and will have fewer turnovers than their opponents. Most turnovers are the result of poor passing decisions and are the bane of offensive basketball, since a turnover robs you of an opportunity to score. Good passing can keep the defense shifting, perhaps to the point at which they cannot keep up with the ball, allowing for a dribble-drive to the basket.

Passing consists of two elements: technique and judgment. The first involves the mechanics of throwing a pass and is relatively easy to teach, given the drills that follow. Passing judgment, on the other hand, is the most elusive art in the game, because it takes into consideration so many variables: circumstances, personnel, and timing, to name a few. A good pass is not only one that can be caught easily,

PASSING DOS AND DON'TS

Do:

- Pass away from the defender.
- Use ball or pass-fakes before passing.
- Make the easy pass. Don't get fancy when the situation doesn't call for it.
- Use bounce passes into the low post.
- Make passes short and crisp.
- Use peripheral vision—keep all options open.

Don't:

- "Telegraph" your passing intent. Be coy and use pass-fakes.
- "Float" your passes. Have some zip on them.
- Jump and then look for passing options.
- Throw to a voice.

FIGURE 8.6
Chest pass

but one that can be converted into an opportunity for the receiver. Just because a pass *can* be completed doesn't mean it's a good one. Knowing *when* to pass is a skill few players possess adequately; it is best developed over time through decision-making drills and scrimmage/game situations.

The five basic types of passes are:

1. Chest pass
2. Bounce pass
3. Two-hand overhead pass
4. Step-around bounce pass (for use into a low post player)
5. Lob pass (for use into denied low post player)

The technique for both the two-hand chest pass and the two-hand bounce pass is the same. The difference is in where the pass is directed. For the chest pass, the player's hands should be behind the ball, with thumbs pointing back toward the body. (See figure 8.6.) She should stride forward with one foot while snapping the wrists forward, thumbs to the floor. The player follows through with arms extended toward the target. *Common problem:* Watch to make sure the player passes straight out from her chest, rather than bringing the ball down to waist level, then back up to pass.

Using the same technique as for the two-hand chest pass, the two-hand bounce pass aims the ball at the floor about two-thirds of the distance to the receiver. The receiver should catch the pass at about waist-high level. (See figure 8.7.) Bounce passes are slower than chest passes but are often the best option when defenders are closely guarding. *Common problem:* Be sure that the person throwing the ball does not bounce the ball too close or too far away from the receiver.

Although the primary error in throwing the bounce pass is the point at which it hits the floor, it is better to err on the side of bouncing it too close to the receiver than too far away. A pass that bounces too soon has a tendency to sit up, bouncing high and making it easy to steal. A pass bouncing too late, or short-hopping to the receiver,

FIGURE 8.7
Bounce pass

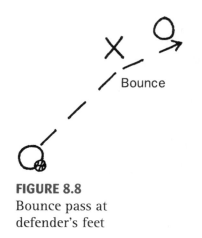

FIGURE 8.8
Bounce pass at
defender's feet

while trickier to catch, is bouncing on line with the defender's feet, making it nearly impossible for the defender to reach down and deflect it away. (See figure 8.8.)

Used to throw over a defender, the two-hand overhead pass is executed with the wrists and forearms. The player places one hand on each side of the ball, thumbs behind. She steps forward to generate momentum and brings her arms forward to flick pass with a snap of the wrists and forearms. (See figure 8.9.) The wrists should rotate forward, with the thumbs ending up pointing at the ceiling. This pass is thrown high and caught high. Overhead passes are often the pass of choice when throwing lob passes or cross-court skip passes.

The step-around bounce pass can be used at any time, but it is most valuable when the passer is being crowded by a defender or when attempting to pass

FIGURE 8.9
Two-hand
overhead pass

from the perimeter into the low post. It is usually used following a pass-fake high. If passing to the right, the player places her right hand behind the ball with her left hand on the side, as in triple-threat position. She then upfakes (fakes a pass high over the top, hopefully getting the defender to reach high to stop it) and steps out to the side with her right foot (the left foot is the pivot foot) to clear the defender. (See figure 8.10.) She should throw low, with a one-hand bounce pass, under the defender with a sort of side-armed motion. *Common problem:* Players often fail to fake high before throwing the pass, making it easier for the on-ball defender to reach out and deflect the pass.

The lob pass describes a *situation* more than a specific *technique,* although the most common lob passes are from the two-hand overhead position. If a low-post teammate is being fronted or denied the ball by her defender, the passer can choose to throw the ball over the top with a pass that leads the receiver to the basket. The receiver should show a target hand, indicating where she wants the pass thrown. The passer should aim 4–6 inches above the target hand, throwing the pass with just a slight amount of arc. (See figure 8.11.) The receiver should hold her position until the ball is directly overhead. She should then release, or jump, toward the ball for the catch. *Common problems:* (1) Passer

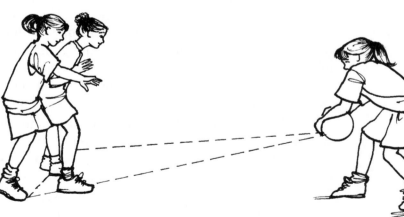

FIGURE 8.10
Step-around bounce pass

FIGURE 8.11
Lob pass

leaves pass too low or too high (use the 4–6 inches above the target hand as a guideline); (2) Receiver gets anxious and releases too early, often resulting in an offensive pushing-off foul.

SHOOTING GAMES

We covered shooting technique in chapter 7. There are an infinite number of drills that a coach can use to work on shooting. Being creative and designing your own drills can be one of the most enjoyable aspects of practice planning. The box "Designing the Perfect

Shooting Drill" offers some tips on the elements that contribute to an effective shooting drill.

INDIVIDUAL OFFENSE

Once your players have some of the basic fundamentals down in terms of footwork, ball handling, passing, and dribbling, it's time to build on those skills and begin developing their offensive game. Earlier in this chapter, we talked about getting open using V-cuts and L-cuts. What follows are some basic offensive moves and situations that can be used once the player has gotten open and received the pass. These can be worked on individually or two-on-two.

PASSING DRILLS

Partner Passing

Involves two players and one ball. Have players line up facing each other, the distance between them dependent on their strength and skill level. Simply have players pass the ball back and forth, starting with chest passes and working through bounce passes, overhead passes, and step arounds. Emphasize stepping through on their passes. After a time, have them use pass-fakes.

Alternative Drills

1. This is the same drill as partner passing, but uses a weighted basketball, if available. After a time, allow players to use a regular ball and listen to the laughter as they begin really zipping their passes.
2. Have players pass against a wall. This is excellent for pure technique work. See how many passes each player can throw and catch in 10 seconds. Make it a competition.
3. Try two-ball partner passing. One player throws a chest pass while her partner uses the bounce pass. Players will get confused once in a while, and balls will collide. Great for the concentration aspect.

Monkey in the Middle

Add a third player to the partner passing as a defender. Have the defenders pressure the passers, trying to get a deflection. This forces the

Jab-Step

The jab step is a basic offensive move that forces the on-ball defender to make a decision on how to guard the ballhandler. From the triple-threat position, the ballhandler uses the free (non-pivot) foot to take a short, crisp jab step at, and slightly to the side of one of the defender's shoulders.

Depending on how the defender reacts, the ballhandler can do one of three things:

1. **Jab-step-and-go.** If the defender does not move to adjust to the jab-step attack, the ballhandler should hesitate a split second

---

passers to use fakes and decide which type of pass to throw. If the defender gets deflection or forces an errant pass, she should exchange positions with the passer. This is also an excellent conditioning drill for the defenders.

Rapid Fire Passing

This is an excellent drill for developing peripheral vision and concentration. Use six or seven players and two balls. One player is the passer with a ball, the others are arranged in a semicircle around her. One of the players in the semicircle also has a ball. Begin the drill with the passer chest-passing to an open teammate while simultaneously receiving a pass from the other person with a ball. This process continues for a pre-determined time span. Emphasize crisp and accurate passes. Increase the speed as comfort levels rise. Passers must be able to see their target while being alert to incoming passes.

Alternative Drills

1. This is the same as the rapid fire passing drill but uses bounce passes or, when very comfortable with the drill, two-hand overhead passes.
2. Rather than arranging players in a semicircle, have them line up straight across, forcing the passer to shuffle laterally up and down the length of the line, adding movement to the challenge.

DESIGNING THE PERFECT SHOOTING DRILL

Guess what? There is no perfect drill for any basketball skill, but there are many good ones, and it's possible that you may be the one to achieve perfection first! Here are some elements of a good shooting drill:

- Keep as many players active as possible. If they're not shooting, they should be rebounding and passing.

- Allow each player to work on shots within her range.

- Work both sides of the floor, so players have the opportunity to shoot from both the right and left sides.

- Give equal time (over time) to catch-and-shoot, off-the-dribble, and bank shots.

- Have players move at game speed and take game shots, so actual game situations are not foreign to them. If they practice at half-speed or take shots they're not likely to see in a game, they are wasting time.

- Most, but not all, shooting work should be of a competitive nature, either against their own standard or with teammates.

SHOOTING DRILLS

Here are some shooting games (as opposed to routine drills) that can be used to liven up your practice and add a competitive element to practice:

+5/−5 Shooting

Have two players per basket, one shooting and one rebounding. The shooter works around the floor, shooting shots in her range. She starts at zero and gets +1 for each make and −1 for each miss. The rebounder keeps track of the score. When the shooter reaches +5, she's shoots two FTs (free throws) before switching to become the rebounder. If the shooter reaches −5, she runs a sprint, then switches with the rebounder.

Knockout

Every player *loves* this game! Form one line at the FT line (or at any spot straight on to the basket). The first two players in line have balls. The first player shoots and must try to make a basket before the second player makes her shot. After the first player makes her shot, she rebounds and passes to the next open player in line. The first player moves to the end of the line and works her way back up. The shooter is "knocked out" if the player behind her makes her shot before the first shooter can score.

Perfect 45

A player shoots from the top of the key (younger players may want to start from the FT line). If she makes the shot, she gets 5 points. The player then attempts a second shot from wherever she rebounds the first shot (off the fly or one bounce). If she makes the second shot, she gets 3 points. The player's third shot is a lay-in with no restrictions. If she makes this last shot, she gets 1 point.

If the ball bounces two or more times before the first shot is recovered, the second shot is null and void. The player may still shoot her lay-up. Each players goes through the sequence five times. A perfect score is 45 points. *Note:* Use two players per basket. Have them alternate until both have gone through the drill five times. This drill not only gives them a variety of shots, but emphasizes following (rebounding) their own shot as well.

Hot Shot

Hot shot is another very popular and well-known shooting game. Begin on the whistle at point B, with the ball. (See figure 8.12.) The player moves around and shoots from the various lettered spots (the point values are in parentheses) for one minute. She must rebound her own shots and can run without dribbling to the next spot, if she so chooses. Shooter receives 3 bonus points if she attempts a shot from all seven designated spots. Only two made lay-ups are counted. Stop on the whistle. If the final shot has been released prior to the whistle, it counts.

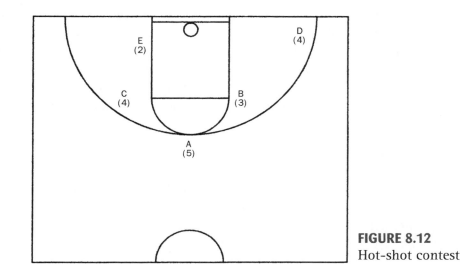

FIGURE 8.12
Hot-shot contest

before attacking in the direction of the original fake. She should dribble hard to get around the defender.

2. Jab-step-and-crossover. If the defender jumps over to cut off the ballhandler upon the initial fake, then the defender has taken herself out of position to defend the drive in the other direction. As the defender moves, the ballhandler pulls her free foot back and across, dribbling hard in the direction opposite the fake.

3. Jab-step, pull-back, and shoot. Once the ballhandler has beaten her defender a few times, the defender will be extra cautious against the drive. When the ballhandler fakes, the defender will not only adjust to one side, she will probably also jump backward to protect against the drive. If the ballhandler is in her range, she simply steps back into the triple-threat position and shoots.

When using the jab-step, players should focus on the defender's front foot (closest to the ballhandler) and attempt to attack the *outside* of that foot. Practice the jab-step using the following series, doing ten reps each:

1. Fake left, drive left
2. Fake left, drive right
3. Fake left, pull-back, and shoot
4. Fake right, drive right
5. Fake right, drive left
6. Fake right, pull-back, and shoot

Be sure that your players work both sides of the floor. Once players are comfortable with the technique, add a defender with instructions to overplay a certain way. This will give the offensive player a point of reference to what she should be looking for when reading her defender. Finally, allow defense to play live, forcing the offensive player to truly read her defender and use the appropriate move.

Post Play

If you have some taller players, they may be more comfortable playing with their backs to the basket in the low post (LP). Rather than try to teach them a series of moves from the LP, let them concentrate on one or two that they can work to perfect.

The drop-step is the foundation of all LP offense. To perform the drop-step, the player should set up on the high side of the block with her back to the basket. This gives her room to make a move in either direction. If she sets up too low toward the baseline, she will have little available room, and the defender can overplay the LP's only remaining option to the middle. With her back to the basket, the post player drop-steps (reverse pivots) to the basket, attempting to seal off the defender's outside leg as she does so. (See figure 8.13.) *Remember:* Teach your players to drop-step to the *basket*, not toward the baseline. If she steps toward the basket, she will seal off the defender, putting the defender behind the offensive post and helpless to defend without fouling. The post player should use one or no dribbles. She should never dribble after receiving a lead pass. If she does dribble, she should use a two-hand power dribble. The post player should step through to the basket, if possible. Otherwise, she should use a power hop, get square, and go up strong.

Similar to the baseline move is the drop-step middle. In this instance, however, the player takes the ball to the middle of the lane area and finishes with a jump hook or a step-through move to the basket. (See figure 8.14.)

FIGURE 8.13
Drop-step baseline

FIGURE 8.14
Drop-step middle

Another move used by the post player is the crossover baseline. In this case, she pivots toward the middle with a shot fake. She then crosses over aggressively and steps through, sealing the defender. She may use a power dribble or step straight through to the basket. The key to this move is a convincing shot-fake and then a quick, powerful move back in the other direction. The player should swing the ball through high and fast while crossing over. (See figure 8.15.)

2-on-2 Play

The give-and-go cut is one of the game's basics, and yet it is used far too seldom. Used properly, it keeps defenders honest, while providing an aggressive scoring opportunity for the offense. This cut to the basket is a read and is effective only when the defender fails to jump to the ball (covered later in this chapter). The offensive player passes to her teammate and starts

FIGURE 8.15
Crossover step (baseline)

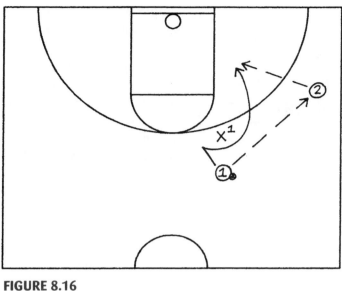

FIGURE 8.16
Give-and-go

away as if to screen off-ball. As the defender relaxes, the player reads her defender being out of position and cuts back hard in the direction of the ball and to the basket for a return pass and an easy lay-up. (See figure 8.16.) This cut is especially effective if your team uses a motion offense that involves constant screening away from the ball.

Five words: John-Stockton-to-Karl-Malone. The pick-and-roll is the simplest play in basketball and, when executed correctly, probably the most effective as well. The problem is that too many youth basketball coaches depend too heavily on this play, to the point where it might be 80 percent of their team's offense. One can understand why it's tempting to do so. Most youth teams, especially the youngest, often appear to be conducting a poorly organized fire drill when running their offense. This is because the game's nuances are still being unfolded for them. Many coaches often give in to the frustration. They have their second-best player set an on-ball pick for their best player, who then dribbles off the pick all the way to the basket while a confused defense tries to figure out how to help. This may result in a score, but if that's all a team does, there won't be much learning going on.

Having said that, the pick-and-roll is still a very effective play and should be one of the first things your players learn beyond individual skill instruction. For purposes of a clear lexicon, the word "pick" refers to a screen set for the player with the ball (pick-and-roll) while a "screen" (covered in chapter 9) is a screen set off-ball.

The pick-and-roll begins with the picker approaching the ballhandler's defender and jump-stopping quite close to the defender. She

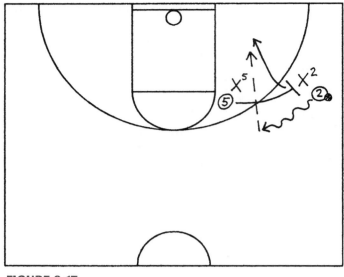

FIGURE 8.17
Pick-and-roll

should have a fairly wide base and have her arms crossed, being careful not to extend her elbows out wide from her body. The pick should be set perpendicular to the defender's shoulder. The dribbler should drive hard off the pick, shoulder to shoulder with her teammate so as not to leave room for the defender to squeeze through and stay with her. The dribbler should look to attack the basket. The picker will maintain her position until the dribbler has gone completely by. Then the picker will *roll* (reverse pivot and cut) to the basket, looking for a possible pass. The dribbler should look to pass to the picker as she is rolling if the picker's defender switches out to help. (See figure 8.17.) *Common problems:* There are several things to look for when teaching the pick-and-roll to your players:

1. Make sure the picker is set up perpendicular to the defender's shoulder.
2. Encourage the picker to hold her position and resist the urge to lean in to the defender as she tries to get by.
3. Make sure the dribbler does not attempt to use the screen and drive to the basket before the pick has actually been set. Otherwise, this could result in a moving pick foul call.

DEFENSIVE SKILLS

Developing a player's individual defensive skills can be a challenge on several fronts. First, defensive play is sometimes less valued by players who gravitate toward the flashy offensive prowess of NBA and WNBA stars. Second, defense is harder to work on individually. It's easy to grab a ball and go shoot around, but it takes tremendous self-discipline to spend an hour on some outdoor court working on defensive slides and shifts.

But defense is more important than offense because defense is more *consistent*. Anyone (and everyone!) can have a bad day shooting the ball. But defense is all about desire and hard work, something that we can muster every time we take the floor. On those days when the offense is struggling, defense allows you to keep the score close and gives you a chance to be successful in the end. We will talk more about team defense in chapter 9, but for now let's look at what the individual player can do to improve her game.

Defense requires that the defender be balanced and in proper position on the court in relation to the ball and the player she is guarding. There are two defensive assignments: on-ball and off-ball. We will discuss off-ball defense in chapter 9. But, before we discuss on-ball defense, I want to touch on one core tenet of off-ball defense—the concept of "On-the-Line, Up-the-Line," hereafter known as OTL/UTL. Also known as the defensive triangle, OTL/UTL refers to the defender's positional relationship with the player she is guarding and with the ball. The "line" refers to the direct passing line between the ball and the player she is guarding. When we say "On-the-Line," we are saying the defender should have one foot close to, or on, that imaginary line or passing lane. "Up-the-Line" refers to the defender being several steps toward the ball, putting her in a position to help a teammate defensively. When playing OTL/UTL, the defender should be able to see both her player and the ball by using her peripheral vision, looking straight ahead and watching for movement out of the corner of her eyes. (See figure 8.18.)

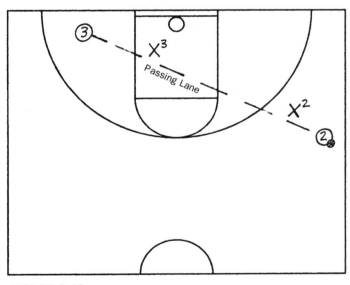

FIGURE 8.18
On-the-line, up-the-line

Denial Defense

When a player is trying to prevent the person she's guarding from catching the basketball, she is said to be "in denial." Defenders should be denying any offensive players who are one penetrating (closer to the basket) pass away from the ball. This means that your players should try to keep the one or two offensive players who are closest to the ball from receiving a pass. Whether denying on the wing or in the post area, the defender should be in a stance approximately facing the offensive player and with her lead arm and hand stretched out across the offensive player's body, palm facing out and thumb down. She should be tagging the offensive player, lightly resting one hand against the torso of the offensive player so as to have tactile contact. Make sure your player doesn't grab or hold, however. As the offensive player moves around to get open, the defender should use retreat steps and advance steps (shuffles) to remain with her player. (See figure 8.19.) Defenders should be aggressive at first.

FIGURE 8.19
Denial defense

If the offensive player consistently beats the defender on backdoor cuts, however, then the defender is overplaying too much and needs to back off a bit. But until that does happen, encourage your players to get out and really pressure the passing lanes.

On-Ball Defense

When guarding a player with the ball, the first principle for the defender is to stay between her player and the ball at all times. The defender should be in a low stance, with her baseline foot slightly back. She should be looking to force any drives in the direction of her baseline foot. The defender should keep her back straight and at about a 45-degree angle to the floor. Her eyes should be glued to the ballhandler's belly and hips, because the ballhandler cannot fake with those body parts. The defender should ignore all head and ball fakes. Where the belly goes, so goes the player.

Defending the Dribbler

The key to defending the dribbler is the defensive slide. This short, quick sideways shuffle that is used to defend the drive must be practiced repeatedly. (See figure 8.20.) Young players will inevitably want to cross their feet when moving laterally, and you will need to spend considerable time working with your players on this aspect of the game. Use a zig-zag drill: Tell your players to get in their defensive stance. Have them slide back at a 45-degree angle. Their first step should be with their lead (directional foot), and then they should slide with the trail foot until it is back in its original position relative to the lead foot. The feet should never come together or cross. After three steps in one direction, have your players switch and go the other way. To change directions, have your players reverse pivot, dropping the trail foot back (drop-step) until it is at a 45-degree angle moving in the opposite direction. Continue to step and slide in this manner.

When defending the dribbler, it is important to stay a half-body-width ahead of the offensive player. Teach your players to

FIGURE 8.20
Defensive slide

think "Nose-on-the-ball." This will put them in good position. Encourage your players to maintain good defensive position and to resist the temptation to reach at the ball.

Defending the Passer or Cutter

Once the ballhandler has picked up her dribble, the defender should apply extreme pressure. Since she no longer has to worry about the drive, she can close up on the offensive player, being careful not to bump or foul her with the body. Encourage your players to trace the ball with two hands rather than waving them furiously. Trace means that they follow the ball with their hands, without touching it. Tell your players to pretend that there is a pane of glass between them and the ballhandler, and they are allowed to mirror the ball, but not break the pane. This will discipline them not to reach in at the ball, where many fouls occur.

If a pass is made, the defender must immediately jump to the ball, establishing herself OTL/UTL and denying a give-and-go cut to her player. (See figure 8.21.)

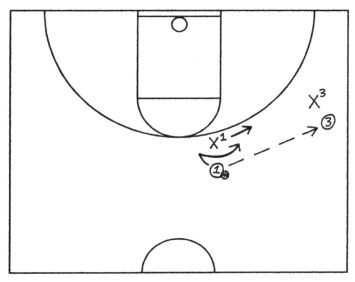

FIGURE 8.21
Defense: Jump to the ball

CARDINAL PRINCIPLES OF GREAT INDIVIDUAL DEFENSIVE PLAY

Teach your players to follow these tips when playing defense:

- Stay low. Keep knees bent. Defenders get themselves in trouble when they stand up or lock out at the knees.

- Stay between your player and the ball (off-ball) or your player and the basket (on-ball) at all times.

- Be On-the-Line, Up-the-Line (OTL/UTL) when playing off-ball.

- Do not allow middle penetration by the dribbler. Force all drives toward the baseline.

- When guarding a player who has not yet dribbled, keep eyes focused on the player's belly and hips, the only area of the body she can't fake with. Where they go, she goes.

- Talk. Don't be shy. Let your teammates know what you are seeing. Communicate.

- Never foul the jump shooter.

Encourage your players to take pride in playing defense. Help them understand that stopping the opponent from scoring two points is the same as scoring two for your team. Any player, no matter her size or speed, can become an effective defender. All it takes is hustle and hard work. Scorers get enough positive reinforcement, believe me. Give as much if not more praise to your players for making a good defensive play as you would for scoring a basket. This will demonstrate your appreciation for their efforts and your commitment to defense.

9

TEAM PLAY

I'VE STATED EARLIER my strong belief that about 80 percent of a youth league coach's practice time should be spent on developing players' fundamental skills. Still, for any young player to continue developing, she will at some point need to transfer those individual skills to a team and game setting. To facilitate this transfer, you will need to spend some of your teaching time on the team principles of offense and defense. But let's keep it simple, okay?

TEAM OFFENSE

If there is one area where many coaches new to youth basketball err, it's in their attempt to install and teach an overly complicated offense. At the youngest age levels, it is difficult for players to remember a complex, structured offense. Youth players should be learning about the *concepts* of offensive play—spacing, how to read the defender, when to pass or drive, good shot selection, rebounding, and screening. Also, as coaches, we should avoid pigeonholing young players into certain positions on the floor. Let your players play several different roles while they are learning.

For these reasons, I strongly believe that a simple *motion offense* is the ideal offense for any youth league team. Variously called "passing game" or "motion," it is predicated on spacing, screening, and reading the defense. There is no predetermined spot for an offensive player to go to at any given moment. She simply evaluates what is happening around her and then reacts. Foolishness, you say? Young players don't understand the game well enough to play a freelance motion? Kids need structure? My answer is a question: Have you ever actually attended a youth league game? From my vantage point, identifying a set offense is pretty difficult. There's a lot of running around, and the teams that are successful are the ones whose players recognize what's occurring around them. These players are learning the *game,* not just an offense. After fundamental skill development, learning the game should be youth leagues' Number Two Goal.

Another reason that motion offenses are great for young players is that they are based on just that . . . *motion!* Young players have a tendency to stand around and call for the ball. This does little to get people open, and eventually the ballhandler takes an ill-advised drive to the basket or forces a pass to a well-defended teammate, often resulting in a turnover. In a motion offense, players learn that if they're standing, they're wrong. Get them to move, anywhere, and you have accomplished something. Get them to move *with a purpose,* and you have taught them something precious.

There are several different types of motion offense, but we will look briefly at two: a basic 3-out motion and its companion, the 4-out motion. But first, let's look at the principles behind any good offense.

PRINCIPLES OF A GOOD OFFENSE

Floor Balance

In youth basketball, the ball is like a giant electromagnet, and the players seem to be wearing metal jerseys. They can't help but cluster near the ball. One of your biggest challenges will be to teach the concept of spacing and balance. By "floor balance," we mean keeping your players spread out. Keep them from bunching up on the floor. Your players should occupy spots on both sides of the floor and should be spaced 12–15 feet apart most of the time. This will keep the defense spread out as well, making it more difficult for the defensive players to help a teammate beaten on a drive to the basket and opening up more lanes for penetration by the dribbler.

Dribble Penetration

More and more, basketball at all levels is becoming one of penetration, or breaking down a defender off the dribble. A strong drive to the basket is one of the best ways to put pressure on the defense. This is especially true of middle (over-the-top) penetration or drives into the lane, or paint. This is because it often forces the inside players to step up and help on the dribbler (inside-out help), thus opening up the players they were initially guarding near the basket. If the dribbler keeps her head up and sees the help coming, she can often pass to her open teammate for an easy shot.

The quicker the player, the better her chance of successfully penetrating past the defense. But even the quickest players must be able to keep their heads up and use good judgment. It is a fine line between being aggressive and forcing it. By forcing it, your players risk turnovers and offensive fouls.

Screening

We discussed on-ball picks (pick-and-roll) in chapter 8. What we want to look at now is screening, the art of an offensive player, without the ball, getting in the way of a teammate's defender and allowing that teammate to cut to the ball for a pass. The defender's path is blocked, and the defender is often late in recovering to the player she was originally guarding.

A successful screen is the result of a good screen *and* a good cut. If not used properly, even the best screens are worthless. Emphasize to your players that screening is a very important job and emphasize to cutters that it is fun to read their defender and make proper use of the screen.

The screening process starts with the screener approaching her teammate's defender at an angle perpendicular to the intended line of the cut. She does this to move into the spot where the screener just came from. By screening at a perpendicular angle, the screener forces the defender to fight over the top or go under the screen rather than simply slide through with the cutter. The screener should jump stop into a balanced stance, arms crossed and elbows in. Once she is set, she cannot move again. She should hold her position until the cutter has cleared the screen, resisting the urge to lean into the defender as she tries to get around the screen and recover. See figure 9.1 for correct and incorrect ways to screen perpendicular to the line of cut.

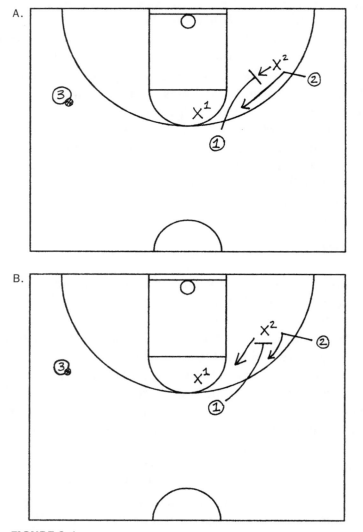

FIGURE 9.1
(a) Correct and (b) incorrect screening perpendicular to the line of cut

FROM THE COURT

The legendary John Wooden had many basketball aphorisms. One of my favorites is, "Be quick, but don't hurry." Jorja Hoehn, four times a women's collegiate National Coach of the Year, always preached to her players that, on offense, "It is better to be late than early." Both coaches meant, essentially, that there's no need to "rush" the offensive part of the game. Encourage your players to relax and let the game "come to them," meaning that they should take the opportunities presented to them, rather than forcing the action.

Cutting

The second part of a successful screen is the cut. The cutter's job is to read the defender and make the proper cut. Cutters must be taught to delay their cuts until the screens are set. Players of *all* ages, but especially young ones, tend to get anxious and want to hurry their cuts. But cutters should be encouraged to s-l-o-w down and wait for the defender to commit to playing her one way or the other. It is at that point that the cutter can make the best decision on which cut to use.

There are four basic cuts that can be made off a downscreen: pop cut, basket cut, curl cut, and flare cut. With the exception of the latter, each cut should be executed with the cutter going shoulder to shoulder off of the screen. There should be no room for the defender to squeeze through with the cutter. We have found when teaching this that the players should be thinking "Nose-to-shoulder."

The *pop cut* is a basic cut, in which the offensive player simply "pops" out perpendicular to the downscreen to receive the pass (see figure 9.2). This is most often seen when the cutter moves to the spot where the screener just came from, replacing her.

If the defender anticipates the pop cut and tries to "cheat" early over the top of the screen, the cutter can make the *basket* (backdoor) *cut*. While not technically using the screen, the cutter nevertheless benefits from the screener's presence, which forced the defender to make a quick decision on how to play the situation. (See figure 9.3.)

If the defender tries to "follow" the cutter over (or around) the screen, the cutter should "curl," or continue her turn around the screen, until she is heading toward the basket. The defender will be

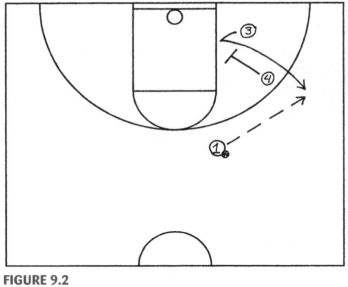

FIGURE 9.2
Pop cut

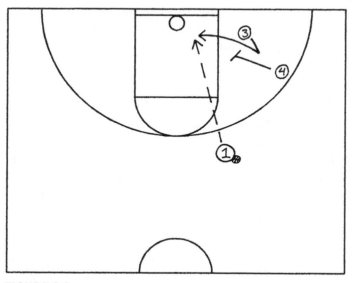

FIGURE 9.3
Basket cut

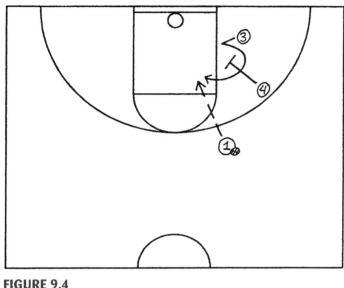

FIGURE 9.4
Curl cut

playing "catch up" and should be out of position to stop the pass and easy basket. (See figure 9.4.)

The *flare cut* is also known as a "fade cut." If the defender tries to go ballside (underneath the screen), the cutter can step back from the screen and look for a skip pass over the top of the screen. As the defender tries to scramble back to her player, she is effectively screened for a second time on the same play. (See figure 9.5.)

For any of these cuts, it is important that the cutter slow down, not rush, and take the time to read how the defender is playing her. An effective teaching point is to have the defender stop—actually stop—and grab the screener's jersey. This will freeze the defender and give the cutter an accurate read of which way the defender wants to go. An explosive cut from there should get her open.

3-Out Motion Offense

The 3-out motion is a very simple offense that operates on the simple premise of pass-and-screen-away. The three perimeter players (point guard, shooting guard, and small forward) will spend most of their time on the outside, screening for each other and using screens set by the posts (power forward [4] and center [5]). They will also look to penetrate when driving lanes are open and will look to pass into the posts when they seal their defender. The posts should generally remain close to the lane area, screening for each other, making cuts from the weakside (the side of the floor opposite where the ball is) to the ball, and screening or picking for the perimeter players. They can

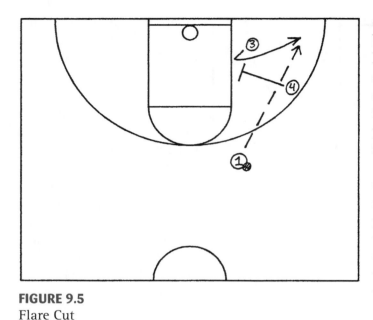

FIGURE 9.5
Flare Cut

occasionally pop outside, but should return to the lane area promptly. They are the primary rebounders and should always be thinking about establishing early position if a teammate shoots. (See figure 9.6.)

Encourage your players to view the offense as a framework. It gives them proper spacing and allows them to operate where they can be most effective. But they should be ready to take advantage of any opportunity that comes along. Keep in mind that offense is jazz, and improvisation is not necessarily a bad thing.

4-Out Motion Offense

The 4-out motion is an effective offense if you have a dominant post player. It gives her plenty of freedom around the lane and provides good driving angles for your perimeter players. The weakness of the 4-out motion is that it is not a great offensive rebounding defense if your players aren't go-getters by nature.

For the 4-out motion offense, your perimeter players should be set up in the four spots indicated in figure 9.7. Players are set fairly high to allow for good baseline drive opportunities. They should focus on pass-and-screen-away, but can sometimes cut toward the ballside, returning to fill a spot and balance the floor if they don't receive the pass. Your post player should be active posting and seeking the ball, but encourage her to mix up her repertoire a little; sometimes staying weakside and screening for players on that side, sometimes waiting weakside before flashing hard to the ball.

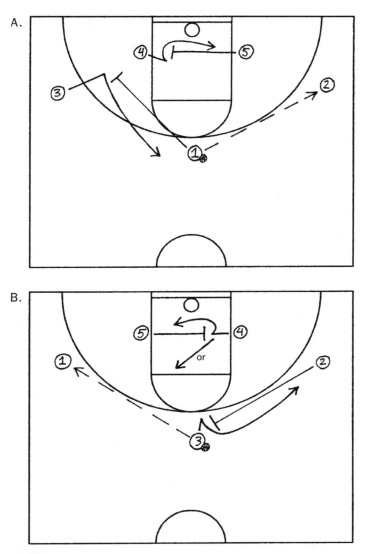

FIGURE 9.6
(a) Basic 3-out motion offense and (b) 3-out motion options

Sometimes she'll come high, sometimes low. She should not let her defender get comfortable

Whatever offense you decide to use, keep it simple, placing your greatest emphasis on spacing, floor balance, and the proper use of screens and cuts. If you do this, you are teaching the *game* of basketball, not just a particular system of play, which, as we said earlier, is one of your primary goals as a youth coach.

Fast Break Offense

Most advanced players *love* to run the floor and fast break. Young players enjoy it, too, but may not completely understand the principles of the transition game and sometimes get themselves into trouble at the end of fast breaks. I don't believe you should spend an inordinate amount of time teaching fast break basketball to youth league players, but it's a good idea for them to practice two of the components that make up true fast break basketball—3-on-2 and 2-on-1 situations. Following is a brief overview of transition basketball, along with a couple of drills that will help you develop your players' instincts for specific situations.

When an opponent's missed shot is rebounded, the rebounder should turn out toward the wing on her side of the court, looking to outlet to any of the perimeter players. The outlet receiver will dribble or pass to the middle of the floor. The remaining perimeter players should fill the outside lanes *wide* and should be sprinting at full speed. (See figure 9.8.) The non-rebounding post, or, in the event that a perimeter player secured the defensive rebound, the first post down the floor sprints rim to rim, running as hard as she can straight down the court. She will eventually post up on whichever side the initial pass goes from the middle of the floor. The middle ballhandler should pull up

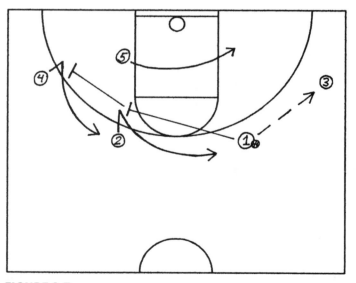

FIGURE 9.7
4-out motion offense

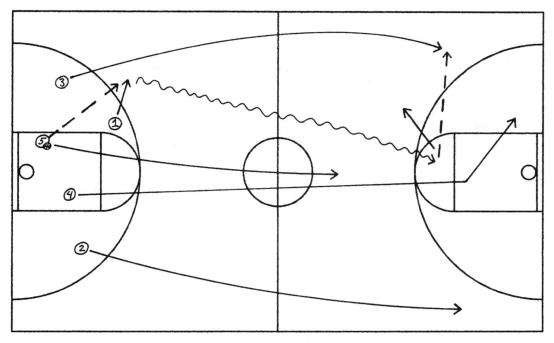

FIGURE 9.8
Basic fast break

THE NOTION OF MOTION

Here are some things to remember when teaching a motion offense:

- Always be moving (with a purpose!). If a player is standing still, she's wrong.
- Keep good spacing, 12–15 feet apart.
- *S-l-o-w d-o-w-n.* Most players hurry too much. On offense, it's better to be late than early.
- Cutters should read the defense and come meet every pass.
- Dribble only to attack the basket or improve the passing angle.

before reaching the FT line and make a decision to pass or shoot. If she penetrates pass the FT line, she will cut down on her passing angles and make it easier for the defense to clog up her options. The "trail"

BUILDING THE PERFECT BREAK

There are many ways to run a fast break, but here are some things common to all successful transition opportunities:

- Get the ball to the middle of the floor as quickly as possible.
- Fill the lanes *wide* to stretch the defense.
- Let the play develop. Players should not predetermine what they want to do.
- Know when you have "numbers."
- Don't penetrate past the FT line unless you're going all the way to the basket.
- Make the easy play. If it's not there, don't force it.

post stays back near the 3-point arc to see what develops and to be a defensive safety in the event of a turnover.

Any time you have more offensive players than defenders at the scoring end, you have a numbers advantage, or "numbers." And any time you have numbers, you should get a good shot opportunity, but the most important thing is to *get a shot*. Because you have numbers for the shot, you also have an advantage on the rebound in case the shot is missed. But you won't have that advantage for long, because the other defenders should be hustling back to help. Let's look at the two most common "numbers" situations, 2-on-1 and 3-on-2.

2-on-1 Situation

In a 2-on-1 situation, the offensive players should be in lanes just wide enough to keep the defender from playing them both. As the two offensive players get inside the 3-point arc, the player with the ball must read the defender. If the defender tries to play it safe and never commits to the ball, or never "takes the basket away" (gets between the ballhandler and the basket), the dribbler should attack the basket for a lay-up. If the defender commits to the ball, the dribbler should pass to a teammate for the easy shot.

3-on-2 Situation

In a 3-on-2 situation, the ball should be in the middle of the floor as the three offensive players approach the basket. If the top defender extends out too far to pressure the ball, a simple pass to the wing will create a 2-on-1 situation with the remaining back defender. (See figure 9.9.) If the defenders lay back initially, the middle person can either shoot or pass to the wing and step ballside, waiting for a possible return pass. If the wing does not have a drive or shooting opportunity, she should pass back to the top, where the point guard (1) will look for the shot or reverse the ball to the small forward (3). (See figure 9.10.) If you have 3-point shooters on the wing, this will be almost impossible to defend.

TEAM DEFENSE

Playing strong team defense involves communication, vision, and proper individual technique. Most youth leagues prohibit zone defenses, so we will not cover zones in this book. What we will examine are the basic principles of man-to-man defense and how they are incorporated into the team concept.

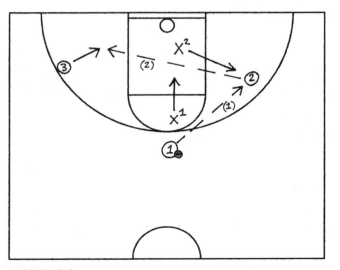

FIGURE 9.9
3-on-2: Scenario 1

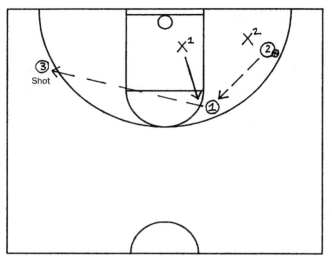

FIGURE 9.10
3-on-2: Scenario 2

3-ON-2 AND 2-ON-1 DRILLS

Here are a couple of good drills for teaching 3-on-2 or 2-on-1 situations:

2-on-1 from Baseline

Form three lines at one end of the court, with the defending line in the middle. On your cue, three players (one from each line) sprint to midcourt. The coach passes the ball to one of the two offensive players. They attack the basket. The defender retreats and tries to protect the hoop.

3-on-2 from Baseline

This is similar to the 2-on-1 from Baseline drill, but with five lines rather than three. The middle line and two outside lines are on offense. Five players sprint and touch midcourt. The coach passes the ball to any of the three offensive players, who then attack the defenders in transition.

3-on-2 to 2-on-1

This combo drill begins with three lines on baseline. Two defenders wait at the far end of the court. The offense attacks 3-on-2. After a score or change of possession, the two defenders are immediately in transition 2-on-1 against the offensive player from the middle line, who gets back on defense.

Players from two outside lines remain as defenders for the next group. This is a continuous drill.

11 Woman

This drill is named for the minimum number of players needed to run it. Players *love* this drill. It is a continuous, fast-paced, 3-on-2 drill. Begin with three attacking two. There should be two outlet lines at each end of the court, as well as two defenders waiting at opposite ends. The offense gets one shot. Make or miss, whoever grabs the ball (it could be any of the five who were playing that 3-on-2 sequence) outlets to one side and then joins the two outlets to form the three-person offensive group attacking the opposite end. Meanwhile, of the four players left behind, two remain on as defenders, while the others replace in outlet lines. (See figure 9.11.) The key to this drill is *one shot*. There are no offensive rebounds or follow shots, just grab the ball and go.

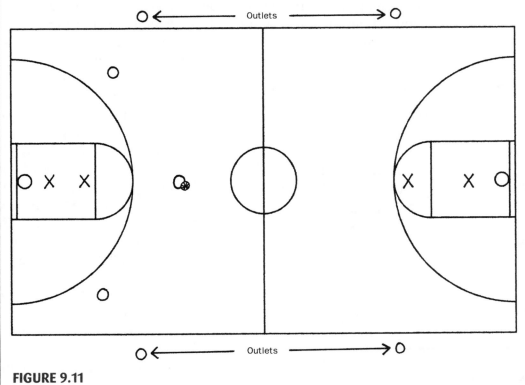

FIGURE 9.11
11-woman drill

We covered on-ball defensive principles in chapter 8, but let's do a quick review of team philosophy. In other words, what do we, as a team, want the on-ball defender to accomplish? The primary objective is to keep the ball on one side of the floor. Force drives baseline (where help is most easily given), and under *no* circumstances do we allow middle penetration.

The four off-ball defenders have a variety of responsibilities (depending on the position of their player on the court), but they *all* must be in a position to help the on-ball defender if necessary. Encourage your players to think in these terms: "I'm responsible for my player and half of everyone else's player, too."

This is a good time to revisit the concept of "on-the-line, up-the-line" (OTL/UTL). Remember that the "line" we're discussing is the imaginary line running from the ball to the defender's assigned player (see figure 8.18, p. 123). Being on-the-line means being in a position to intercept any direct pass to the weakside offensive player. Up-the-line refers to the defender being several steps off her player and toward the ball, putting herself in a position to help defensively.

In figure 9.12, the ball is up top at the start of the offense. Defenders X^2 and X^3 are in a denial position because they are one pass away, meaning their players are the most likely to receive the next pass. X^4 and X^5 are two passes away, and are OTL/UTL slightly.

As the ball moves to the wing, we see now that X^3 is on-ball. X^5 is in low post denial, while X^4, X^2, and X^1 are all helping and are OTL/UTL. (See figure 9.13.)

When the offensive player drives the baseline, X^4 rotates over to help, while X^2 rotates to cover X^4's assignment. (See figure 9.14.) This is called *second-*

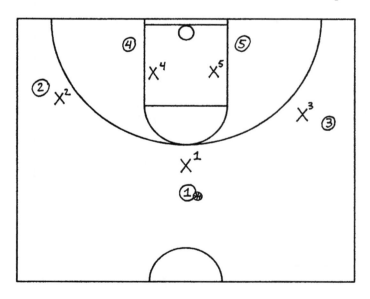

FIGURE 9.12
Defensive positioning: Ball up top

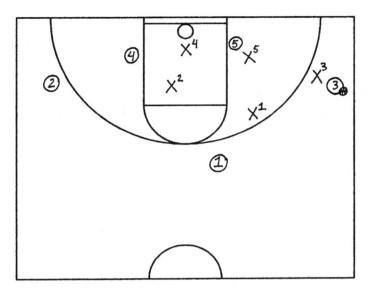

FIGURE 9.13
Defensive positioning: Ball on wing

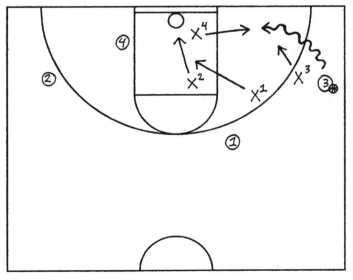

FIGURE 9.14
Help and rotation: Baseline drive

ary rotation and refers to help for the intial help defender. A general rule of thumb on team defense is that on a drive to the basket, all defenders should collapse into the lane and help. The only exception is when you are defending a great 3-point shooter and you may not want to help too far off her unless it's absolutely necessary. If the shot goes up, everyone must block out and rebound. If the ball is passed back out to the perimeter, each defender recovers to her own player.

Defending Screens

Most offenses use screening to get players open to receive a pass. When teaching your players how to defend screens, the most important consideration is *communication*. Your players should be continually talking on defense anyway, but it's doubly important with screens, because the player being screened has two things to worry about: her player *and* the screener.

When an offensive player goes to set a screen, that player's defender should be yelling, "Screen left, Olivia!" or "Screen right, Sparky!" Knowing which direction the screen is coming from gives the defender an extra split-second to evaluate the situation and adjust accordingly. More important, it reduces the chances of your team's players running into blind screens, a sometimes painful and always annoying occurrence.

Coaching Tip

If you have trouble getting your players to talk on defense, try banning it! Play a 4–5 minute segment of shell defense or 5-on-5 scrimmaging in complete silence. Your players will soon realize how difficult it is to play basketball *without* talking!

Defending Downscreens

Downscreens are used to help an offensive player coming toward the ball to get open. In figure 9.15, the offensive wing (2) is setting a downscreen for the post (5). X^5 should clearly be able to see the screener approaching, but X^2 should still yell out, "Screen, right!", step back off her player toward the ball (open up), and assume a position OTL/UTL. This gives X^5 room to slide through the gap (called going ballside, as opposed to following the cutter around the screen) and deny the pass to 5 on the wing. In calling out the screen and giving room for her teammate to slide through, X^2 has worked with X^5 to defend the screen successfully. *Common problem:* X^2 fails to back off her player while she's screening, thus failing to provide a gap for X^5 to slide through, and, in fact, effectively setting a double-screen on her own team-mate. (See figure 9.15b.)

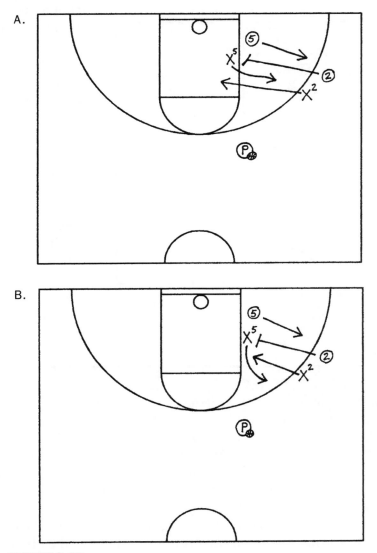

FIGURE 9.15
Defending the downscreen: (a) Correct and (b) Incorrect

Defending Cross-Screens

A cross-screen is essentially a downscreen set on a lateral plane. The purpose is the same: to bring an offensive player to the ball for a pass. This is most often used in the post area, but all of your players

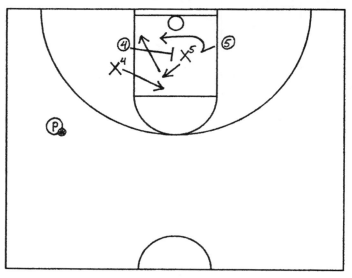

FIGURE 9.16
Defending the cross-screen

should understand how to defend this screen. As one post cross-screens for another, X^4 should communicate to X^5 that a screen is coming. X^4 is now in an OTL/UTL position. X^5 steps up over the screen ballside and then through the gap between X^4 and the screener, denying the cutter low. (See figure 9.16.) (*Note:* If the cutter goes high, the screen is not being used, and X^4 will simply deny her player in the normal manner.) Some

DEFENSE DRILL (SCREENS)

With the coach as a passer up top, the offensive wing downscreens for the post. (See figure 9.17a.) X^2 calls out the screen and opens up, allowing X^4 to slide through. The coach passes to the offensive wing. At this point, the posts cross-screen. (See figure 9.17b.) X^4 yells out the screen and stays OTL/UTL. X^5 steps up over the screen and slides through the gap into low post denial. The offensive wing passes back to the coach up top. Everything is back at the beginning, with the players in different starting spots. (See figure 9.17c.) This is a continuous drill in which the offense is not trying to score. When you first run this drill, have the offense move slowly and be prepared to stop the action often to give instruction.

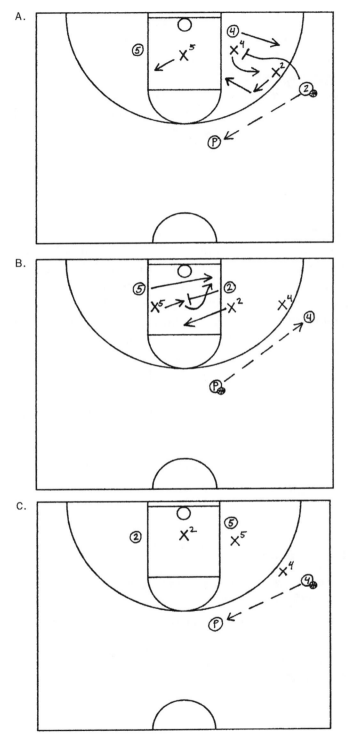

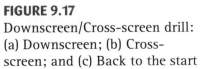

FIGURE 9.17
Downscreen/Cross-screen drill:
(a) Downscreen; (b) Cross-screen; and (c) Back to the start

common problems: (1) X^4 doesn't call out the screen soon enough for X^5 to react in time; or (2) X^5 doesn't step up over the screen quickly enough and is successfully screened.

After your players have come to understand the principles of defending the downscreen and cross-screen, have them try the drill on page 148, which combines the two and includes wing denial defense.

Defending On-Ball Picks

One of the trickiest defensive situations to master is defending the pick-and-roll, or on-ball pick. Communication here is critical. Quite often, the defender on the ball is extremely focused on defending her player and is not necessarily employing her peripheral vision as she would if she were playing off-ball, or help, defense. Therefore, it is critical that the screener's defender start calling out the impending pick early, loudly, and often. "Pick right, Jorja! Pick right, Jorja! Pick right, Jorja!" As the dribbler begins to use the pick, X^5 steps out, staying low, and hedges, forcing the dribbler to take a momentary path away from the basket. X^3 should fight over (follow) the pick and recover to a spot between her player and the basket. X^5 recovers back to her player (screener), who is likely rolling or cutting toward the basket. (See figure 9.18.) *Common problems:* (1) The screener's defender steps out too late or at too shallow an angle, and the dribbler is able to go around her to the basket, as shown in figure 9.19a;

THREE REASONS NOT TO SWITCH ON SCREENS

1. Switching on defense can make defenders lazy. If they know they don't have to fight over or through screens, their intensity may diminish.

2. Switching may result in mismatches, with a smaller player having to guard a bigger player. This may be trouble near the basket.

3. Unless team communication is excellent, switching against a fast-paced offense can be confusing, leading to major breakdowns that leave a player wide open.

FIGURE 9.18
Defending the pick-and-roll

or (2) The dribbler's defender tries to go underneath the screen and gets caught up on the screener rolling to the basket. This often results in a switch, with a guard now defending a post cutting to the basket (see figure 9.19b).

Keep in mind that team defense is not easy to execute. It requires hard work, commitment to each other, and, most of all, communication. Encourage your players to take pride in themselves defensively as a team. There is no greater symbol of teamwork.

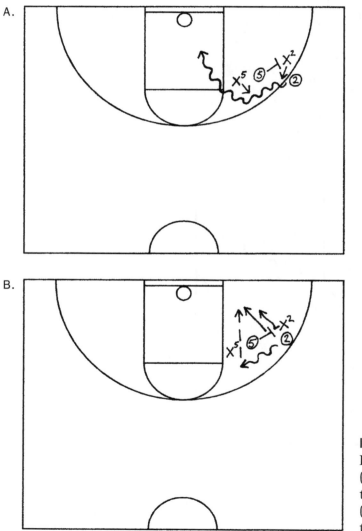

FIGURE 9.19
Pick-and-roll defense:
(a) Help defender steps out too shallow; and
(b) Dribbler's defender tries to go underneath pick

10

OTHER COACHING AND BASKETBALL SITUATIONS

YOU'RE PROBABLY AWARE by now that there are countless aspects of the game that need to be addressed, in addition to the offensive and defensive fundamentals of basketball. Practice time is limited for most youth teams, and it is often difficult to cover everything you'd like to. (In this book, I have purposely omitted discussion of zone defenses, zone offenses, presses, and press offenses, because most youth leagues do not allow them.)

In this final chapter, we start with a very important element of basketball, rebounding, and proceed to touch on jump ball situations and inbound plays. Finally, we briefly discuss game coaching responsibilities and how to provide your players with the best possible game-day experience.

REBOUNDING

Simply defined, a rebound (or "board") is the retrieval of a missed shot attempt, either an opponent's or your own. Of the three possible ways to gain possession of the basketball (the two others are turnovers by the opposing team and letting the opposing team score), *rebounding* is the most desirable method. Rebounds are superior because turnovers by the other team are too infrequent and letting the other team score is never a good option! Keep in mind that rebounding is both a defensive and an offensive skill. Every defensive rebound ends the offensive team's chance to score. Each offensive rebound is like an extra possession and an additional chance to score.

Blocking out, or *boxing out,* means getting between the player you are defending and the basket and establishing contact. The player blocking out should place her rear in the opponent's gut and stay low ("sit down") while keeping her hands up at about shoulder level. The defending player can create contact either by using a forward pivot and stepping into the opponent, or by a reverse pivot (often used to cut off an opponent who is trying to go around her to get to the basket). Once contact is established, the defending player should stay low and move laterally, as necessary, to maintain the block out. (See figure 10.1.)

Coaching Tip

Most drills are designed to work on and improve defensive rebounding techniques. But don't ignore offensive rebounding. Your youth team will miss many shots. A young player's instinct is to stand and watch the ball, as I like to say, to spectate, when a teammate's shot goes up. Encourage your players to react early and chase down those misses.

As the missed shot comes off the basket, the player should jump *to* the ball. She should avoid trying to reach out and bring the ball back to her body. Advise her to rip the ball down to about chin level and protect it by extending her elbows, as shown in figure 10.2. This gives her a strong grip on the ball. A common problem for many young players is a tendency to bring the ball down too low, to waist level, where they are often tied up for a jump ball.

FIGURE 10.1
Blocking out

FIGURE 10.2
Post-rebound position

When first introducing rebounding, spend a good deal of time working on the technique of blocking out. Once your players have a grasp of how to create and establish contact, you can move on to more integrated drills. Finally, you should make a point of carrying the technique work over to scrimmages and games. In "live" situations, most young players will turn to watch the ball when it is shot rather than look for someone to block out. You will need constantly to remind them to find their player and "put a body on her!"

REBOUNDING DRILLS

Here are some effective drills that you can use:

Ball-in-the-Middle

This is a fun way to learn the basics of blocking out and holding position. A ball should be placed on the floor in the middle of the half-court center circle. Have four or five pairs of players stand around the outside of the circle. "Defenders" start from the inside position. When the coach blows a whistle, offensive players try to be the first one to touch the ball. The defensive players try to keep them out. Defenders need to create and maintain contact, riding the offensive player wide of the ball. How many seconds can they maintain the box out until someone breaks through to touch the ball? Kids love this drill!

2-on-2 Rebounding

This simple drill works for both offensive and defensive rebounding. It can be given different looks by moving the lines to two different spots on the floor. The coach shoots, and on the release, players yell, "Shot!" while stepping to make contact with the offensive player. Coaches should limit offensive movement at first to allow the defenders some early success. After a time, let them play live. If offense gets the rebound, they try to score. If defense gets ball, have her throw an outlet pass. Offense rotates to defense, and defense rotates to outlet position. Outlet receivers move to the end of the opposite line. (See figure 10.3.) *Note:* Coaches can make this a competition, if they choose, by dividing into two teams and awarding 2 points for an offensive rebound, 1 point for a made basket (or for being fouled in the act of shooting), and 1 point for a defensive rebound.

Rotation Rebounding

This drill can be done 3-on-3 or 4-on-4. In figure 10.4, players are set up on both blocks and in the middle of the lane. Two shooters (usually coaches) are at midwing and begin skip passing back and forth. Meanwhile, the three defensive players must continuously rotate (coach chooses the direction), each calling out the name of the player she would be responsible for blocking out (which, obviously, changes every second or two) if the shot were taken that instant. Eventually, the coach shoots, at which point the offensive players may attack offensive boards. Defenders must establish contact and block out.

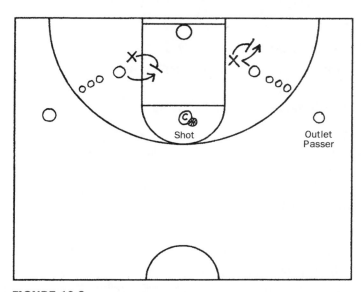

FIGURE 10.3
2-on-2 rebounding

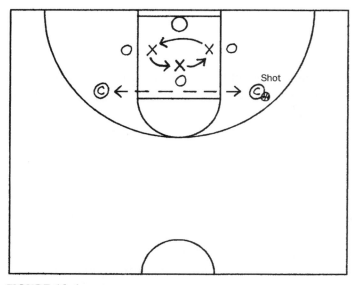

FIGURE 10.4
Rotation rebounding

BOARDING BASICS

Here are some basic principles of rebounding to emphasize with your players:

- Always assume every shot will be a miss. Work hard to establish good position under the basket.
- Most missed shots carom off to the opposite side of the basket.
- Shoot long, rebound long.
- On defensive boards, always make contact with your player (block out) and stay low. Keep your hands up at all times.
- On offensive boards, crash the gaps (open lanes) to the basket. If blocked out, spin or roll off the defender in order to get by her.
- Jump to the ball. Don't try to reach out and gather it in.
- Keep the ball high after securing it. Bring it to chin level and protect it with elbows out.
- The offensive player with the best chance to grab a rebound is the shooter. She knows earlier than anyone how the shot may miss (short, long, left, or right), and very few defenders do a good job blocking out the shooter.

SPECIAL SITUATIONS

Jump Balls

Jump balls, generally, are used only at the start of a game; you won't need to devote much time to them. Figure 10.5 illustrates a basic defensive jump ball alignment. The key is to make sure you can protect your basket initially if the opponent secures possession off the jump.

Inbound Plays

Far too few teams take advantage of this tactic. When putting the ball in play from underneath her own basket, the player should not be content with just getting the ball inbounds. Your plays should be designed to create a quick and easy scoring opportunity. Keep things simple. Try running two or three different plays from the same set. That way, the defense will not be able to guess the play from the for-

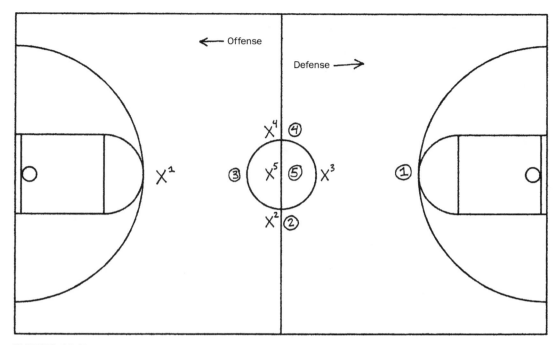

FIGURE 10.5
Basic defensive jump ball alignment

mation. You might also wish to have nonverbal cues for the plays you run. You might run three different plays out of a "box" set, and they can be designated by having your point guard stand with her feet together, apart, or staggered. Just make sure your players know to look and see which option is being "called."

Figures 10.6 and 10.7 give you two options. Figure 10.6 shows two options for line inbound play, and figure 10.7 shows two options for box inbound play.

COACHING THE GAME

All of that hard work your players have put in at practice finally gets displayed come game time. At the higher levels of play (high school, collegiate, and professional), game coaching is often a series of strategic moves and countermoves. However, in youth basketball, the

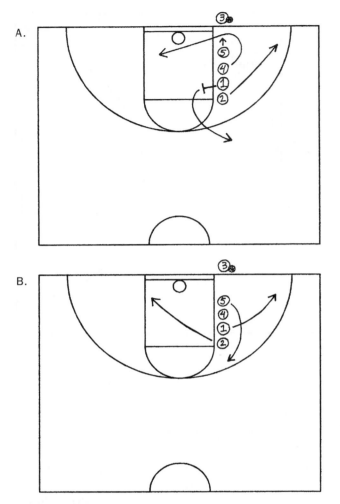

FIGURE 10.6
"Line" inbound play: Option A and Option B

emphasis during games should be on learning and effort. Your job as coach is to facilitate an enjoyable experience for your players and to help them continue to learn about the game.

If your league doesn't have an equal playing time rule for the youngest age groups, it should. At ages 7–9 or so, there should be little emphasis on winning, but great encouragement given to playing hard and playing together as a team. As players get older, win-

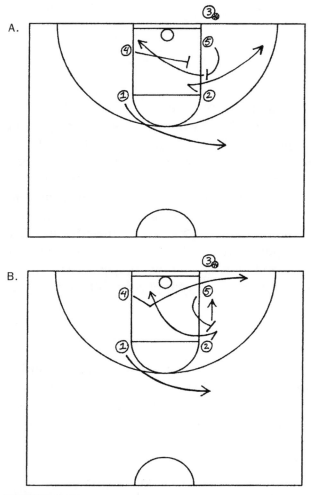

FIGURE 10.7
"Box" inbound play: Option A and Option B

ning and losing become parts of the experience, but even then playing well should be your primary goal.

Use games as a teaching tool. When you substitute for a player,
take her aside briefly and let her know what she was doing well and
what she can do better next time she goes in. Reassure players who
may be frustrated. Do not chastise them for mistakes, but, instead try
to help them correct whatever the problem is. The only time you

should show disapproval should be for a lack of effort or displays of poor sportsmanship.

Conduct

As coach, you set the example for your players to follow. Therefore, your conduct must be exemplary. When you interact with your players, do so in a calm and composed manner. Your players will be tuned in not only to what you say, but also to how you say it. If you are positive and caring, the feedback you give will be absorbed more readily.

But nowhere is your behavior more important than in your conduct toward the referees. If you get caught up in the officiating and start complaining, your players will begin to lose their focus. Most youth league officials are young, often high school aged kids. They are not professional referees, and you should not expect them to be. Demonstrate respect for the officials, and your players will do the same.

Pregame Talk

Youth league game preparation does not include lengthy scouting reports on the opposing team and discussion of specific ways to counter their strengths. At least, it shouldn't! Focus your pregame discussion on what you want your players to accomplish: play good

---

MAKE THE MOST OF TOUR TIME-OUTS

During a time-out, you have a limited amount of time to get your point across. Here are some tips for effective time-outs:

- Make sure the entire team can hear what you are saying. All players need to know of any changes you may make.
- Keep your message brief and simple.
- Discuss only one or two points, the most important one last.
- Focus on what you want the players to do, not on what they're failing to do. Be positive.

defense, set good screens, block out on the defensive boards. Give your players just two or three things that you're looking for them to do. And remind them to have fun.

Half-time

Coaching Tip

When diagramming plays, orient the board to face the same way as the current court set-up. Keep your diagrams consistent with the baskets you are attacking and defending, minimizing any confusion about instructions.

Think of half-time as an extra-long time-out. After talking with your assistant coaches about what you'd like to accomplish in the second half, approach your discussion with the team positively, telling them what you'd like them to accomplish. Don't waste time pointing out negatives. For example, if you are being badly outrebounded by your opponent, tell your team, "We need to do a good job blocking out during this half. Make it a priority to establish contact on every shot." As in a time-out situation, give your players one or two things to concentrate on doing. Ask if they have any questions, and then let them go warm up for the second half.

Postgame

Win or lose, don't try, immediately following the game, to analyze the contest. I've found that coaches inevitably feel differently the following day. You'll realize that you played neither as well nor as poorly as you thought you did right after the game. So, find something to compliment your team for, reconfirm when the next practice or game is, and send them off for postgame munchies. And as they walk away, thank your lucky stars that you have the opportunity to coach these young ladies. Your responsibility is a profound one, but it is also deep in rewards. Savor the opportunity.

APPENDIX: RESOURCES

THE INTERNET TODAY OFFERS a wide array of Web sites devoted to any and all aspects of coaching youth sports. These sites vary wildly in quality, breadth of content, and stability (Web sites seem to come and go in a flash). The sites listed below are good jumping-off points. Many are directed at those working with youth sports. Some are devoted to basketball at all levels. Most have a "links" button that can direct you to related sites. Explore for yourself and see which sites you find useful!

American Sport Education Program (ASEP)
www.ASEP.com
A commercial site offering educational courses and resources for coaches, directors, and parents.

Coach's Clipboard
www.homestead.com/BbplaysDrills/index.html
A wide variety of selections on drills, offenses, defenses, and fundamentals. Also has a section on the "mental game." An excellent resource.

Coach's Notebook
www.alaskalife.net/sjordan/notebook/indexn.html
Another fine site aimed at volunteer coaches. Has a little bit of everything.

Human Kinetics
www.humankinetics.com
This long-standing clearinghouse for physical education teachers has a wide variety of book and video titles dealing with all aspects of sport and fitness.

InfoSports.Com
www.infosports.com
Basketball section of this multi-sport site has many coaching articles presented in a semi-bulletin board format.

Institute for the Study of Youth Sports
ed-web3.educ.msu.edu/ysi/
Based at Michigan State University, this site offers a variety of coaching resources and links. Features a "Bill of Rights" for young athletes.

165

National Alliance for Youth Sports

www.nays.org

Organization dedicated to making sports safe and positive for America's youth. Links for coaches, parents, and kids!

North American Youth Sport Institute

www.NAYSI.com

Commercial site providing general coaching education materials.

Positive Coaching, Inc.

www.PositiveCoaching.org

Committed to educating youth league coaches and parents. Emphasis is on putting the athletes first.

The Locker Room

members.aol.com/msdaizy/sports/locker. html

Oriented toward kids. Basketball section offers information on the history and rules of the game and fun facts about basketball. There's also a glossary of terms and a wonderful section on teaching the various fundamental skills of the game.

Tom Lynch's Basketball World

www.geocities.com/Colosseum/Stadium/6330/

Aimed at youth coaches. Emphasis is on developing shooting skills, but site includes essays on developing a youth program and the philosophy of youth sports.

Total Coaching.Com

www.totalcoaching.com

At this site, not only will you find articles on basketball here, but you'll also be able to look at various approaches to conditioning, nutrition, and fitness.

Ultimate Youth Basketball Links Page

www.worldofsports.com/links.htm

"Ultimate" is their claim, not my endorsement, but it is an excellent list of links related to all things basketball.

YouthSports USA

www.ysusa.com

A sprawling, multi-sport behemoth of a site dedicated to all aspects of youth sports. Takes some time to navigate, but there's something here for everyone.

GLOSSARY

Arc   The trajectory of the ball when shot at the basket. There are three types: low, medium, and high.

Backdoor cut   (*See* Basket cut.)

Ball handling   The process of moving the basketball around the court, usually by passing or dribbling.

Bank shots   Shots that carom off the backboard before entering the basket. Also known as shooting off the glass.

Basket cut   Offensive move in which the offensive player moves behind the defender to the basket to receive a pass. Also known as backdoor cut.

Blocking   Bumping and physically impeding a moving player.

Blocking out   Getting between the player being defended and the basket and establishing contact. Also known as boxing out.

Bounce pass   A pass in which the ball is bounced off the floor and to the receiver.

Boxing out   (*See* Blocking out.)

Breakdown drill   Plan for coaching basketball skills by deconstructing a skill or play into parts.

Center   Usually one of your taller players who plays with her back to the basket and is skilled at catching, passing, and shooting. Also known as post player.

Change-of-pace dribble   Varying the height or the speed and rhythm of a dribble to keep a defender off balance.

Charging   An offensive foul in which an offensive player with the ball runs into or displaces a defensive player who has established position.

Chest pass   A pass in which the ball handler gets the ball to another player by throwing the ball straight out from the chest.

Control dribble   The basic dribble move when closely defended. Bounce the ball close to the body and low to the floor.

Crossover move (low post)   Offensive move in which the post player pivots toward the middle with a shot fake and then crosses over aggressively and steps through, sealing the defender.

Crossover dribble   A dribbling move that switches the ball from one hand to the other in front of the body. Used to change direction with the ball.

Cross-screens   Interior screen, usually from low post to low post, designed to free up a post player for a pass near the basket.

Curl cut   An offensive player, sensing the defender trying to follow her around a screen, curls hard around the screen and to the basket, leaving the defender trailing.

Cutting   The process of moving into position to receive a pass.

Defensive slide   Short, quick sideways shuffle that is used to defend the drive.

Denial defense   Defensive technique in which a player is trying to prevent the person she is guarding from catching the basketball.

Double dribbling   Illegal move in which a player dribbles the ball with both hands at the same time or begins dribbling the ball after having picked up her initial dribble.

Downscreen   Play used to help free up an offensive player who is coming toward the ball.

Dribble penetration   Breaking through the defense by dribbling hard to the basket.

Dribbling   Bouncing the ball with one hand while moving the ball around the court.

Drop-step   Offensive move in which the low-post player sets up on the high side of the block with her back to the basket. This allows the player the chance to move in either direction toward the basket by performing a reverse pivot (drop-step).

Fade cut   (*See* Flare cut.)

Fast break offense   The offensive team moves the ball quickly downcourt in an effort to attack the basket before the defense can set up.

Five-second rule   A violation in which an offensive player holds the ball for more than 5 seconds, without passing or dribbling, while being closely defended. Also applies to an offensive player inbounding the ball, as they need to do so in a short time span.

Flagrant foul   A violation that is called when unnecessary force is used or when a player's safety is put at risk.

Flare cut   An offensive move used by an offensive cutter when a defender tries to go ballside. The cutter steps back from the screen and looks for a skip pass over the top of the screen.

Floor balance   Keeping players spread out on the court, rather than clustering around the ball.

Fouls   Violation in which illegal contact is made.

4-out motion offense   An offensive set that uses four perimeter players passing, screening, and cutting, and one interior post player positioning near the basket.

Free throws   An uncontested shot that a player makes from the free-throw line following certain types of fouls.

Front pivot   Stopping and then turning one foot forward while keeping the other foot on the floor at all times.

Full-court pressure defense   The concept of playing defense tightly all the way down the floor, with hopes of forcing the offensive team to rush and lose control of the ball or force a poor shot.

Give-and-go cut   A basic basketball skill in which the ball handler passes to a teammate and makes a quick cut to the basket for a return pass and an easy lay-up.

Hand-checking   Impeding the progress of the dribbler by placing the hand on the body and pushing or holding.

Holding   A non-shooting foul in which a player grabs or restricts another player's movement by using the hands or arms.

I-cut   Changing direction on the court by moving back and forth on the same line. Ineffective in getting open.

Illegal screen   Foul that occurs when a screener is not completely set or stationary when the contact with the screened defender is made. Also known as a moving screen.

Inbound plays   Putting the ball in play from outside the court.

Jab-step   Basic offensive move that forces the on-ball defender to make a decision on how to guard the ballhandler. The ballhandler uses the free foot to take a short, crisp jab step at and slightly to one side of the defender's shoulder.

Jump ball   Usually used only at the start of the game. Two players face each other in the center of the court. The referee tosses the ball straight up in the air between the two players, who then jump up and try to pass the ball to their own team.

Lay-ups   A shot in which the ballhandler takes off close to the basket and jumps explosively and releases the shot toward the backboard at the height of the jump.

L-cut   Offensive move in which the cutter takes the defender toward the ball and then cuts out to the side at a 90-degree angle to receive the pass.

Lob pass   A pass used if a low-post teammate is being fronted or denied the ball by her defender. The passer opts to throw the ball over the top with a pass that leads the receiver to the basket.

Motion offense   A team offense of constant movement predicated on spacing, screening, and reading the defense.

Non-shooting foul   A foul that occurs outside the act of shooting.

Off-ball   Position of defensive players who are not guarding the ball.

On-balance   The attribute of having equal weight distribution between both feet.

On-ball   Defensive player(s) who are guarding a player who has the ball.

On-ball picks   (*See* Pick-and-roll.)

On-the-line/up-the-line   Refers to the defender's positional relationship with the player she is guarding and with the ball. "Line" refers to the direct passing line between the ball and the player being guarded. On-the-line means the defender should have one foot close to, or on, the imaginary passing lane. Up-the-line means the defender should be several steps *toward* the ball, putting her in a position to more readily help a teammate defensively. Also referred to as OTL/UTL and the defensive triangle.

Over-and-back violation   Retreating into the backcourt with the ball after having crossed the midcourt line.

Over-the-back foul   A rebounding foul in which an offensive player runs into or displaces a defensive player who has established position.

Palming   Carrying the ball by getting the palm of the hand underneath the ball and turning it over on the dribble. Also called carrying. This is a violation.

Passing   Throwing the ball to another teammate.

Perimeter players   Players who play facing the basket.

Pick-and-roll   Setting a pick on the defender guarding the ball and then rolling, or cutting, toward the basket after the dribbler goes by. One of the easiest, most effective offensive plays for getting the ball past a defender.

Pivot   To change direction by keeping one foot on the ground at all times.

Plyometrics   A form of conditioning designed to increase explosiveness and jumping ability.

Point guard   Player who is the best passer and dribbler; often responsible for running the offense. Usually a shorter, faster player who is able to penetrate defense.

Pop cut   Basic cut in which the offensive player simply jumps out, perpendicular to the downscreen, to receive the pass.

Post player   (*See* Center.)

Post up   To get good offensive position near the basket.

Power forward   A bigger, stronger player who is able to rebound at both ends of the floor. Must enjoy the physical aspects of playing near the basket.

Progressions   Teaching method in which players learn the basics of the game and then proceed to more and more complex skills.

Pull-back dribble   To dribble the ball back toward the body while the player backs up on the court to get out of traffic.

Rebound   The retrieval of a missed shot attempt, either the opponents or your own.

Reverse dribble   While dribbling, the ballhandler reverses pivot and cups the ball, pulling the ball back and around to the opposite side.

Reverse pivot   Stopping to change direction by keeping one foot on the ground at all times and turning backward.

Screens   An offensive player, without the ball, gets in the way of a teammate's defender and allows that teammate to cut to the ball for a pass.

Secondary rotation   How remaining defenders react and move when a teammate has helped initially on a drive to the basket. The remaining defenders must rotate toward the basket to cover the newly exposed offensive openings.

Shooting foul   Occurs when an offensive player is fouled while attempting a shot at the basket. Two or three free throws are awarded.

Shooting guard   Often the best outside shooter on the team. Also known as the two-guard or the off-guard.

Shooting off the glass   (*See* Bank shots.)

Small forward   Hybrid offensive position combining the shooting and ballhandling skills of a guard and the rebounding prowess of a post.

Speed dribble   Dribble the ball high and push it out in front to sprint down the open court with the ball.

Step-around bounce pass   A ballhandler upfakes (fakes a pass high over the top) before stepping out to the side and passing the ball to a teammate.

Technical foul   A foul called against a player or coach who shows bad conduct during a game.

3-out motion offense   A simple offense that operates on pass-and-screen-away principle. Three perimeter players spend time on the outside, using screens set by posts and by each other. They look to penetrate when driving lanes are open. Meanwhile, posts cut and screen for each other.

Three-second lane violation   A violation that occurs when a player stands in the lane at her offensive end of the floor for more than three consecutive seconds.

Tracing   Defensive technique of following the ball with both hands, without touching the ball in the offensive player's hands.

Transition basketball   (*See* Fast break offense.)

Traveling   A violation that occurs when a player takes more than one step without dribbling the ball.

Triple-threat position   From one position or stance facing a basket, a player is able to pass, drive (dribble), or shoot.

Two-hand overhead pass   A pass that is used to throw the ball over a defender.

Turnovers   Occurs when the offensive team loses control of the ball to the defending team.

V-cut   Offensive move in which the cutter cuts for the ball on a different line than the one she used for setting up the defender.

INDEX

The author and Prima Publishing extend a special thank you to the El Dorado Hills girls' basketball team, The Lakers, for taking time out of their day for a photo shoot. Grateful acknowledgments to coaches Jeff Look and John Brenan for rounding up a team of girls to be photographed for the book cover. And thanks to the spirited team players (from left to right): Samantha Look, Katie Muhr, Erin Brenan, Lauren Hardison, Holly Ginter, and Sloan Magee.

ABOUT THE AUTHOR

Sandy Simpson, a former player for the University of California, Davis, Aggies, started his coaching career while still a student at U.C. Davis. In 1977, he began a five-year stint as an assistant under former Aggie's coach Pam Gill-Fisher. He graduated in 1981 with a bachelor's degree in history. Simpson then moved to the University of Washington coaching staff for three years, while doing graduate work in kinesiology. He later served on the George Washington University coaching staff for a year, and then assisted Washington State in 1990. During all the moving around, Simpson continued to help out throughout the 1980s at the UC Davis Girls' Basketball Camp.

In 1991, Simpson rejoined the Aggie program, after spending a year as head coach of a First Division professional team in Germany. In 1997, while serving as interim coach of the U.C. Davis women's basketball team, Simpson guided the team to a program-best 29-3 record, a Northern California Athletic Conference (NCAC) championship, and a third-place finish in the school's first-ever trip to an NCAA Division II Elite Eight basketball tournament. The Aggies finished the NCAC season with a perfect 14-0 record, and Simpson was named the NCAC Coach of the Year. In 1999, after his team posted its sixth straight 20-win season, Simpson was named the California Collegiate Athletic Association (CCAA) Coach of the Year. His success as an interim coach made his selection for head coach on June 1, 1999, a logical one. Since returning to the Aggies, he has been a part of 210 wins, seven league titles, and eight NCAA Tournament berths. Currently in his fifth season as head coach, he owns an 87-26 record overall.

Simpson and his wife, Chris, live in Dixon, California, with their daughter, Olivia, and their son, Sebastian.